Ghosts and Legends of the Merrimack Valley

Ghosts and Legends of the Merrimack Valley

CC CAROLE

Published by Haunted America
A Division of The History Press
Charleston, SC 29403
www.historypress.net

Copyright © 2009 by CC Carole
All rights reserved

First published 2009

Cover image by Bob Abagis.

Manufactured in the United States

ISBN 978.1.59629.747.0

Library of Congress Cataloging-in-Publication Data

Carole, CC
Haunted Merrimack Valley / CC Carole ; forewords by Susan J. Caldwell and
Laura Kimberley.
p. cm.
Includes bibliographical references and index.
ISBN 978-1-59629-747-0 (alk. paper)
1. Haunted places--Merrimack River Valley (N.H. and Mass.) I. Title.
BF1472.U6C354 2009
133.109742'72--dc22
2009034978

Notice: The information in this book is true and complete to the best of our knowledge. It is offered without guarantee on the part of the author or The History Press. The author and The History Press disclaim all liability in connection with the use of this book.

All rights reserved. No part of this book may be reproduced or transmitted in any form whatsoever without prior written permission from the publisher except in the case of brief quotations embodied in critical articles and reviews.

*To my husband, Robert, who keeps me strong and focused.
I love you.*

CONTENTS

Forewords, by Susan J. Caldwell and Laura Kimberley	9
Acknowledgements	13
Introduction	15
History of the Merrimack River Valley	19
Native American Legends	23
Witches	31
Sleep Tight	39
Restless Structures	53
Table for Two	63
Haunted Mills and More	73
Underground Railroad	85
Over the River and Through the Woods	95
RIP	101
References	107
About the Author	109

FOREWORDS

When CC Carole asked me to write the foreword for her book *Ghosts and Legends of the Merrimack Valley*, I was honored and excited to be a part of this latest venture of hers. One of her best qualities—and I think the one I admire most—is fearlessness. Whether she is crawling through dark, enclosed spaces following a spirit or performing a Lucy and Ethel–like skit on a ball field to promote a TV show, she is committed to providing her personal best. Nothing seems to get in her way. I am certain that she has attacked this most recent task with the same commitment to excellence and that it will be a thoroughly enjoyable experience.

I met CC in 2005, when she was introduced to me by a client of mine. CC was coproducing *Ghost Stories of New England*. I was looking for local inspirational women to interview for *Applaud* magazine, which I created in 2003 for New Hampshire women. I think what spoke to me first was CC's positive energy and enthusiasm for everything. I decided right away that I needed to make her the cover story of our next issue, naming her the Inspirational New Hampshire Woman in the fall/winter of 2005.

CC brings a unique gift to the ghost hunting genre—her ability to communicate with spirits. This new genre has recently become very popular, with several shows dealing with exploring haunted locations.

Forewords

Although other ghost hunting groups have sophisticated equipment, they do not have CC's capabilities of communication, nor is freeing spirits within their scope. CC has a passion for soothing the souls of the departed. She credits her grandmother for this gift and feels that this is what makes her viewpoint special.

New England is one of the oldest areas of our country and is rich in history. Much of this history has come about from acts of violence, either from people or from the environment. This creates a multitude of haunting opportunities and souls in need of soothing. I am sure this book is just the beginning of CC's sharing of her unique experiences with her readers.

Please keep your eyes open because I think you will find CC in another fall issue of the newly transitioned *Applaud Women*.

Susan J. Caldwell
Owner/Founder
www.ApplaudWomen.com

There is a lot to be said of a deep soul that questions, thinks and endears to others its learning. In beautiful forms of expression, CC Carole ("CC the Huntress") has done just that in both the past and the present. She has endeared her views to hundreds, if not thousands, with her steady, raw insight into all things past, present and future.

We here at IPAA (International Paranormal Acknowledgment Awards) and PNT (Paranormal Television Network) express great pride and honor in CC the Huntress's nomination in many award categories for her sincere dedication to history, the paranormal and seeking the unknown. We are also proud to have her paranormal television shows aired on PTN. CC has been a true pioneer in her efforts, going forward to where not many women in today's world dare trod. She leads future generations along a wide path

Forewords

to continue humankind's quest for the unknown. She is a true individual. Sincerity and truth run through her veins, and I am proud to call her my colleague and friend.

Laura Kimberley
Director of the IPAA
www.ipaawards.org
Executive Producer of PTN
www.paranormalnetwork.com

Acknowledgements

First and foremost, I would like to thank my husband, Robert, whose love for me has never waned. He is gracious, generous, kind and a loving father to our children. Through the diversity life has thrown at us, Robert has remained the one solid rock of our family. I thank him from the bottom of my heart for all he has done and continues to do.

I thank my husband and children for accompanying me on my travels during the research of this book.

Thank you to my beautiful daughter Laurel for the pictures she took for this book. Her knack for creative photography astounds me. She was my sounding board and a true asset in the making of this volume.

I thank my son Bobby for the pictures taken for my book and for having a special sense for working with the paranormal. His direction and video ability made the early projects of *Ghost Stories of New England* into *CC the Huntress* for national TV. Because of Bob's filming, our DVDs are quite the hot items!

I heartily thank my son George, who has the biggest heart of any person I've known. He is always ready to help as a crew member on our paranormal shows and is never afraid to venture into haunted places. George also helped with the catchy titles of the chapters and pictures in this book.

Acknowledgements

To Bobby and Danielle, my loving son and daughter living so far away, I thank you for being the bright and beautiful stars you are. I always get a giggle when I think of the time we ran through that graveyard with the authorities hot on our trail. I love your laughs and smiles and miss you dearly.

Introduction

I was honored and delighted when asked by The History Press to write a book on the history and ghostly hauntings of the Merrimack Valley in New England. I proudly titled my book *Haunted Merrimack Valley*.

I have lived in New England just about all my life. The Merrimack Valley is extra special to my heart, as I spent my adolescent years wandering down its old country roads and riding through its fields on horseback. I investigated abandoned houses deep in the woods to see if the stories I heard about ghosts haunting them were true. Sometimes the buildings were haunted, and sometimes they weren't.

I have always been fascinated by the rich history and exciting stories of ghosts, spirits and the paranormal that surround the Merrimack Valley. This book gives me a chance to blend the two subjects I love in an educational and entertaining fashion.

Each chapter's contents have been fully researched for historical accuracy. I have also fully investigated the locations for paranormal and ghostly activities and healed the spirits with which I came into contact.

As you read *Haunted Merrimack Valley*, know that I have traveled to each and every location to see and experience for myself the magnificent history and the ghostly stories. What I did not want to do was create a catalogue of so-called hunted places similar to other ghost books on the market. I wanted you to be able to visit

Introduction

and investigate these places on your own. The locations in this book may surprise you.

You will read about Native American legends. These legends, mixed with historical facts, are so important to our valley's and our country's history. They actually paint a beautiful picture in our minds of the incredible Native American joy for life and the afterlife they so creatively embraced.

You will experience true tales of witchcraft based on the witchcraft hysteria that took place in Salem, Massachusetts, in 1692. Did you know that there were more witches accused of witchcraft in Andover, Massachusetts, a town in the Merrimack Valley, than in Salem? It's true!

Our roots along the Underground Railroad are uncovered within these pages. For the most part, the Merrimack Valley supported the abolishment of slavery. The residents of the Merrimack Valley provided a safe haven in their homes for the newly arriving travelers of the Underground Railroad in the hope that they would reach their goal of freedom farther north. To this day, sounds are heard, and strange, dark, shadowy figures have been reported in and around the areas of the safe houses and tunnels.

Historic homes, inns, taverns and buildings fill the towns that make up the awesome Merrimack Valley. Many make you feel as though you have taken a step back in time. Their antique rooms and grounds cry out with untold stories of days gone by. Some say these cries can still be heard.

Lining the banks of the mighty Merrimack River are the early industrial mills of our beautiful valley. They were the life force for the many people who depended on them for their livelihood. From the stagecoaches of the thriving Concord Coach Company in Concord, New Hampshire, to the bustling shoe mills of Haverhill, Massachusetts, most products were made in these mills. The Merrimack River, like other mighty rivers, powered the mills with sheer water energy. One could say they were green before their time. The mills of the Merrimack Valley employed thousands of hardworking people during their heyday. They also experienced life and death within their walls.

Old graveyards tell of the lives and deaths of the persons buried beneath. Graveyard art is one subject that never ceases to amaze me. It shows the ever-changing growing faith we have in our belief systems,

Introduction

be they Christian, pagan or in between. Views of death, dying and the afterlife are portrayed in the art found on and in old graveyards. The old graveyards of the Merrimack Valley are no exception. The Matthew Thornton Graveyard in the town of Merrimack, New Hampshire, is the final resting place of one of the cornerstone signers of our country's most honored document, the Declaration of Independence. Much can be inferred about this great man by what is so eloquently written on his gravestone. His headstone was marked by a simple inscription: "The Honest Man."

Our intricate trails and smaller waterways, such as the canals that serviced the mills, still offer a glimpse of the people and animals that ventured along their routes. Animal trails turned into Native American pathways and then into dusty dirt roads for farming settlers. They now stand abandoned for the more progressive roadways and highways of modern times. The old roadways were once essential to the growth and prosperity of our farmers and the running of the mills. Many say these trails and waterways are now mysteriously silent; some even say they are haunted.

If I have left out your favorite haunted place, don't worry. I'm in the process of writing many more books on the subject! I hope you enjoy my book and learn some fun ghostly facts along the way.

HISTORY OF THE MERRIMACK RIVER VALLEY

Where It All Began

To understand the full depth and magnitude of the historic Merrimack Valley, one must first gain an understanding of the river for which the valley was named—the Merrimack.

The mighty Merrimack River got its name from the Pennacook Indians of southern New Hampshire and the North Massachusetts region. The word *Merrimack* means "sturgeon." The sturgeon was a fish in great demand by the Native Americans who lived along the Merrimack River. It populated the waters of the Merrimack in abundance. The Pennacook Indians, knowing the importance of the river for life and food, named it appropriately. In 1604, Pierre Dugua, Sieur de Monts, an explorer from France, was forging his way to Archia (Nova Scotia). He was told by local Native Americans of a mighty river to the south. This river was the Merrimack.

The Merrimack River is 110 miles (177 kilometers) in length. It starts at the junction of the Pemigewasset and Winnipesaukee Rivers in Franklin, New Hampshire. The Merrimack takes a southerly journey through New Hampshire and Massachusetts. When it reaches the city of Lowell, Massachusetts, it takes a northeast course and joins the Atlantic Ocean at Newburyport, Massachusetts. Its total watershed is 5,000 square miles (1,295 kilometers). Its elevation is 280 feet (85 meters), and its coordinates are latitude 43°26'11° north, longitude 71°38'53° west.

The mighty Merrimack. *Photo by George Abagis.*

In the beginning, before the Ice Age, the Merrimack River took quiet a different course as it traveled to its final destination. Its course ran relatively southerly and straight until it reached Boston, at which point it joined the Atlantic Ocean. After the Ice Age, part of the original Merrimack River was filled in with dirt and debris from the receding glaciers. Thus, the current course of the Merrimack was created.

The word *Merrimack* had many different spellings over the years, partly due to the fact that some of the settlers of the area did not have proper schooling and they tended to spell phonetically. Different variations include: Merrimacke, Merrimac, Marrymac, Merimacke, Merimack and Merrymake. It is clear from these variations that a legal standard was necessary.

The spelling of the name Merrimack was settled once and for all in 1914, when U.S. Congressman John Jacob Rogers of

Massachusetts asked the State of Massachusetts for a uniform spelling. It was granted, and the legal spelling of both the river and valley became Merrimack.

The Merrimack Valley is made up of cities and towns spread between two states—New Hampshire and Massachusetts. From Concord, New Hampshire, to Haverhill, Massachusetts, and including all of the cities and towns in between, each city and town is filled with its own unique history and pride, and its own diverse and distinct appeal. Despite individual differences, one common bond remains intact and in full view—the life force of the mighty Merrimack River.

The Merrimack Valley has seen it all, from glaciers to Native American and Pilgrim settlements to wars and present-day industry. It has also seen its fair share of paranormal activity, or, in laymen's terms, ghosts. The Merrimack Valley is haunted by the ghosts and spirits of its previous dwellers.

Native American Legends

Proud and Beautiful People

When one thinks about Native American legends, one might think about the easy, carefree life and romantic tales of a beautiful people. In this chapter, I hope to bring a few of those mystical tales and legends to life. Our country's foundations and our forebears' survival in the New World would not have been possible without the gracious and kind acts of Native Americans. Their history is rich, their legacy spans time and their souls are pure.

Unlike romantic tales, history shows a trail of hardship traveled by Native Americans of the Merrimack Valley. By reading the history I have set forth before you, I hope you will come to cherish, as I have, the mystical tales and legends of the Native Americans of the Merrimack Valley.

The Merrimack River Valley, from Concord, New Hampshire, to Haverhill, Massachusetts, was primarily the home of the Pennacook Indian tribe. The Pennacook Confederacy encompassed a large group of tribes and villages located along the entire length of the Merrimack River and beyond. They are respectfully noted as follows: Accominta, Agawam, Amoskeag, Coosuc, Nashua, Newichawanoc, Ossipee, Pawtucket, Pennacook, Pentucket, Piscataqua, Souhegan, Squamscot, Wachuset, Wamesit, Weshacum, Winnecowet and Winnipesauki. Pennacook comes from the Abenaki Indians, who were located east of New Hampshire's White Mountains in the state of Maine. The name *Pennacook* means "at the bottom of the hill." They were most likely named for the location of their villages along the Merrimack River. This coincides with the bottom of the White Mountains.

Because of their location inland, the Pennacooks had little or no contact with European settlers of the New World before 1620. Even without contact with the new settlers, the Pennacooks were not without their own major unnamed epidemics. One such epidemic occurred around the time frame of 1564 to 1570 and another around 1586. These epidemics took their toll on the entire population by spreading rapidly with deadly consequences.

In about 1603, the Penobscot and Micmac tribes were skirmishing over who would do business with the French fur traders in Acadia. These steady skirmishes soon heightened to the point of all-out war, called the Tarrateen War (1607–1615). They fought the battles of the Tarrateen War all the way into eastern Massachusetts. While in eastern Massachusetts, the Micmac tribe ran directly into a band of European slave raiders. What the Mimacs encountered was far

The dying.

Passaconaway, chief of the Pennacooks.

more deadly than any battle or war they had fought to date. They were infected with deadly diseases that spread at a highly aggressive rate. After the war, the Micmacs returned to their native lands in the north, bringing the deadly diseases with them. Not one tribe in the Merrimack Valley and north, including the Pennacooks, escaped the devastation that the diseases left in their wake. Three-quarters of the entire Native American population succumbed to the rampant spread of disease.

It was estimated that in 1563 there were at least twelve thousand Pennacooks in thirty villages in and along the Merrimack Valley. By the time the European settlers arrived in 1620, the Pennacook population numbered about twenty-five hundred. This reflected a devastating loss in population. The Pennacooks were again hit hard in 1631 by the smallpox epidemic, which started along the Merrimack River. It quickly spread into a full-blown epidemic in

New England during the time frame of 1633 to 1635. By 1639, it had returned at full strength. Influenza followed in 1647, and then smallpox again from 1649 to 1650. Diphtheria struck in 1659. At this point, the Pennacook population dwindled to fewer than twelve hundred people.

The Pennacooks had a brilliant and powerful chief who ruled from 1620 to 1660. His name was Passaconaway, meaning cub, papoose bear or child of bear. Passaconaway was born sometime between 1550 and 1570 and died in 1679. He would have been over one hundred years old. It is said that Passaconaway had magic powers. He could make water burn and trees dance. It was passed down through the generations that Passaconaway could take a dried-up dead leaf and turn it green. He was also said to be able to bring a dead snake back to life. He is noted throughout history as being one of the first chieftains to lease land to the new settlers. He made his home at the beginning of the Pawtucket Falls in Lowell, Massachusetts. A statue of his image was erected there in 1935. In later years, he moved north to Merrimack, New Hampshire, to an area known as Horseshoe Pond. For those familiar with the Daniel Webster Highway in Merrimack, New Hampshire, Horseshoe Pond is directly across the street from a tasty ice cream stand called King Cone.

During Passaconaway's rule, he made it a point to try to get along with the new settlers. In one case, it was reported that he handed over to the English authorities one of his own relatives. This relative, while intoxicated, murdered a white male settler. In 1660, Passaconaway passed his rule to his son, Wonalancet, who later passed it to Passaconaway's grandson, Kancamagus. When Passaconaway died, it was said that a sled pulled by a wolf pack brought him over Lake Winnipesaukee to the top of a mountain. At the top of the mountain, there was a fiery explosion that catapulted Passaconaway to heaven.

King Philip's War (1675) was a two-year battle between the Native Americans and the English colonists. To date, it is considered one of the bloodiest wars ever fought in America. The war was over the growing settler population and the fact that the Native Americans were being pushed out of their native lands. By the end of King Philip's War, the population of the Pennacooks had taken a drastic drop to a mere five hundred or so people. This was not due to the war but to ongoing disease. In fact, not all of the Pennacook tribes fought in the war; only the Nashua and Wachusett tribes were involved. Pennacook chief Wonalancet upheld his father's beliefs of getting along with the new settlers.

As time went on, frustration built. Even with the Pennacooks' devastatingly low numbers, the tribe teamed up with the Abenakis in 1689–97 for what is called King William's War. This was the first of the French and Indian Wars. The Pennacooks and Abenakis traveled south into New England to seek revenge on the new settlers. The French and English armies fought over the rights and ownership of the colonies.

The New England colonies had a rather loose and voluntary—as well as short-lived, from 1686 to 1689—agreement with England regarding protection from the French and Native Americans. Dominion Governor Edmund Andros took charge of the settlers' land and opposing land deeds and put a stop to town meetings. He also tried to force the Church of England down the throats of the American settlers. Upon hearing that King James II was overthrown and William of Orange was the new king of England, the settlers rebelled and had Edmund arrested on May 18, 1689. The dominion was no more.

By the time Queen Anne's War ended in 1713, the Pennacook Indians were no longer in existence. The handful of Pennacooks remaining were absorbed by the Abenaki tribe. It was said that their extinction as a tribe was more in name than in fact. The following passage is from an article on the First Nations Histories website:

> *According to the New England version of the story, there were still a few Pennacook along the upper Merrimack in 1719. By 1726, there was a single village near Concord, New Hampshire, with only five men, and before they "rode off into the sunset," the "Last of the Pennacook" saved some of the colonists from starvation that winter. All of which was probably true regarding this one group, but the Pennacook themselves had not disappeared. For that matter, neither had the Pocutuc, the Nipmuc, the Abenaki, or the other tribes that New England history had found convenient to declare extinct. They continued as the St. François Indians, the Bcancour Abenaki, and the Vermont Abenaki. Although often*

thought of as Canadian Indians and French Allies, they were, in fact, the original residents of New England.

I have included here a few of the colorful and mystical tales and legends of the Pennacook Indians. I took these delightful stories from the pages of two special books: *Legends of Yesterday* (Standard Book Company, 1919), by G. Waldo Browne; and *Myths & Legends of Our Own Land*, volume one (J.B. Lippincott Company, 1896), by Charles M. Skinner. I did not want to compromise the mystique of these stories, so they appear exactly as they were printed in those books. They are precious and of great historical value.

Passaconaway's Ride to Heaven

One winter night the howling of wolves was heard, and a pack came dashing through the village harnessed by three to a sledge of hickory saplings that bore a tall throne spread with furs. The wolves paused at Passaconaway's door. The old chief came forth, climbed upon the sledge, and was borne away with triumphal apostrophe that sounded above the yelping and snarling of his train. Across Winnepesaukee's frozen surface they sped like the wind, and the bleated hunter shrank aside as he saw the giant towering against the northern lights and heard his death-song echo from the cliffs.

Through pathless woods. Across ravines, the wolves sped on, with never slackened speed, into the mazes of the Agiochooks to that highest peak we now call Washington. Up its steep wilderness of snow the ride went furiously; the summit was neared, the sledge burst into flames; still there was no pause; the height was gained, the wolves went howling into the darkness, but the car, wrapped in sheaves of fire, shot like a meteor toward the sky and was lost amid the stars of the winter night. So passed the Indian king to heaven.

I traveled to the top of Mount Washington to look for paranormal activity. According to the story, Passaconaway took flight to heaven from the summit of Mount Washington. With my scientific energy measuring meters, I proceeded to document the area, looking for fluctuations in energy.

Ghost hunters measure the electric energy levels with various tools. If the energy moves, let's say, five degrees one way, this might indicate a ghost nearby.

With my heat meter, I measured negative twenty degrees to positive fifty-six degrees. This was the largest jump I have ever recorded. The outside temperature was a mere thirty degrees. The energy level fluctuation was so intense that it led me to believe that something very big had happened here. I asked the great leader Passaconaway if I could perform a healing. His reply was a request that I say a prayer for the Pennacooks. After receiving this message, I said a prayer for comfort and prosperity and prayed that the Merrimack Valley would never forget the contributions of the Pennacooks. After my prayer, I tested the area again to see if the energy levels still fluctuated. They did not. They stayed constant at thirty degrees. To me, this trip and healing were complete successes.

The Moose and the Fly

Many, many moons ago the moose were plenty about here, and in that distant day their leader was king of all creatures of the wildwood. He was so great in form that two men, standing upon the other's shoulders, could not reach the back of this monarch of the forest. The valley of the Merrimack was his favorite resort, and as he frequently drank from the river, which ran unvexed by rocky barrier from highland to sea, he looked triumphantly over all that came within range of his vision.

It so happened that he came hither one day from a race with such an enormous thirst that while he quaffed the cooling beverage it seemed to those who looked on that he would never stop. So long and so deep did he drink that the beaver called to his companions out of fear lest the great river should be drained of its last drop, and they spake to the other creatures, until it was known to all that it was being swallowed up by this thirsty monster.

The poor fish began to scurry hither and thither to find some pool which might possibly escape this mighty drinker. Then one, bigger and wiser than the rest, sent a fly to alight upon the moose.

Angered by the attack of this little enemy and unable to dislodge the tiny pest which was pushing him so severely, the moose tossed high his head and stamped the ground madly with his great hoof. Lo! In the twinkling of an eye, a great change took place. Behold! The river that had flowed so smoothly was suddenly broken into fragments and sent headlong down rocky stairways, and so swiftly did it run away from him that no longer could the thirsty creature endanger its life.

The Pennacooks gave the falls the name of *Kasgonshadi*, simply worded, "river of broken waters." The story is set at the Amoskeag Falls in Manchester, New Hampshire, the tallest of the falls on the Merrimack River. The moose was the tallest of all moose. The Amoskeag Falls have a drop of fifty feet (fifteen meters). As time went on, the falls were called *Nasmoskeag* by the Pennacooks, meaning "place of good fishing." And indeed it still is.

The Amoskeag Falls are not far from where I live. My daughter Laurel attends college in one of the newly renovated mills that line the Merrimack River, and we set off to visit the falls, not so much to look for paranormal activity but to get a grasp of the magnitude of this awesome creation. While I don't believe that the moose stomping his hoofs created the falls, the story reflects the romantic notions of which legends are made. We lowered our heads in silent recognition of this magnificent design.

WITCHES

Not Just for Salem

When one thinks of witches, one probably thinks of Salem, Massachusetts. I think of Andover, for two reasons. First, Andover, Massachusetts, is part of the Merrimack Valley and Salem is not. Second, Andover—and this is not a well-known fact—had more people accused of witchcraft during the witch hysteria than any other town in New England, and that includes Salem.

In 1688, Reverend Samuel Parris was invited by John Putnam, an elder of Salem Village, to visit the area and preach in Putnam's church. Reverend Parris liked the area so much that he accepted an offer to stay and become the village minister. Parris's family included his wife, Elizabeth, their young daughter, Betty, and a slave called Tituba. Though she was thought to be a Negro slave, Tituba was born in a small Arawak village in South America. As a child, she was sold into slavery and brought to Barbados. Reverend Parris purchased Tituba to work for his household when she was about thirteen.

In the winter of 1692, Betty Parris began to act strange. Some blamed her behavior on the extremely cold February weather. After a few months, Betty's playmates started to act strange as well. They threw themselves onto the floor, convulsed and said vulgar swearwords to anyone who came near them. A diagnosis was quickly made by Cotton Mather, minister of Boston's Old North Church. He said that a curse had been placed on the girls by a witch. He proclaimed himself

The stock for punishment. *Photo by Bob Abagis.*

an expert on the subject of witchcraft, for in 1689 he had written a book called *Memorable Providence*, which told the story of Mary Glover, an Irish washerwoman who bewitched four children of Boston Mason John Goodwin. Betty and her playmates—Ann Putnam, Mercy Lewis and Mary Walcott—were, in Mather's mind, acting out in the same manner as the Goodwin children.

On February 25, 1692, Tituba's neighbor, Mary Sibley, offered a remedy of rye cake mixed with Betty Parris's urine to be fed to a dog. The belief was that the dog would take away the curse placed on the girls because dogs were believed to work directly with the devil. The remedy didn't work, and the list of girls affected by the curse grew. When asked for the name of the witch who had placed the curse on them, they named Tituba, Sarah Good and Sarah Osborn. Arrest warrants were issued for the three women on February 29, 1692.

In time, the list of accused witches grew so large that the jails were filled to capacity. On May 27, 1692, Governor Phips ordered that a new court be held for the witchcraft trials, duly called the Court of Oyer and Terminer. Cotton Mather and three of his best friends were appointed to the new court by then governor Phips. On June 2, 1692, Bridget Bishop was the first accused witch to be tried. Bridget was a tavern owner. Many in the town had been upset with Bridget before she was accused of being a witch because she operated her tavern, which served apple cider ale, on Sunday.

The girls traveled to towns throughout the commonwealth of Massachusetts, rooting out and accusing witches as they went. Stories of flying devils in the midnight air and pinches from witches caused such a stir that townspeople began to confess that they had seen these witches flying through their homes. They believed the girls' statements, and the accused witches were forced to confess or be put to death.

Increase Mather, father of Reverend Cotton Mather, along with other people of high social standing, wanted to put an end to the hysteria that had taken over Salem Village. In August 1692, he wrote a book called *Cases of Conscience*. His main argument was that it "were better that ten suspected witches should escape than one innocent person should be condemned." The book came out on the same day his wife was to be named a witch.

Increase Mather took his arguments to the courts and asked that they not include spectral evidence and touch testing when judging a person on trial for witchcraft. Spectral evidence was evidence based on dreams and visions, and touch testing was a test used by the accuser to see if the accused was really a witch. The test was performed with the accuser's eyes covered. The accused was led in front of the accuser and asked to touch the accuser's shoulder. If the accused was really a witch, the accuser would scream, drop to the floor and convulse. If the accuser did nothing when touched, then the accused was not a witch.

Mather presented his argument to Governor Phips. In October 1692, Governor Phips ordered the courts to use only accurate and convincing evidence when ruling in cases of witchcraft. This ruling came in a timely manner given the fact that the governor's wife, Lady Mary Phips, was named as a witch. As a result of the new ruling, the remaining twenty-eight accused witches were not convicted. Three were pardoned, and the rest were released from jail.

By the end of October 1692, nineteen people had been convicted of witchcraft and subsequently executed. Four of the accused died in jail awaiting their trials. There was also the case of eighty-year-old Giles Cory, who was accused of witchcraft in April 1692 and would not admit to guilt nor claim innocence. Because he stood mute, he was sentenced to be pressed to death. He was the only sentenced witch to be executed in this most horrific and painful manner. It took two days for Giles Cory to die. Robert Clef, who witnessed the death, reported that the sheriff pushed the dying Cory's tongue back into his mouth with his cane. To this day, no one knows where Cory's unmarked grave is located.

It is said that the jails were filled with about two hundred people charged with witchcraft and awaiting trials. Two dogs were executed for being linked to the devil.

There are recognizable names of the accused, convicted and executed, like Rebecca Nurse and John Proctor, and there are lesser-known names, like Roger Toothaker and Lyndia Dustin. The same can be said of the towns. We all know about Salem, with its witch museums and sightseeing tours that illuminate the witchcraft trials. We also know the name of the official witch of Salem, Laurie Cabot. But we often forget Andover, the town that was hit the hardest during the witch hysteria.

It all started with Andover resident Joseph Ballard and his loving wife, Elizabeth. In July 1692, Ballard became extremely worried about his wife because she had been sick for so long. He believed that her sickness was the work of the devil through witchcraft. He had heard of Ann Putnam and Mary Walcott and how they could tell if someone was a witch, or better yet, if someone was bewitched and by whom. He sent for the girls to examine his sickly wife and to give him the names of the witches in Andover.

Ann Putnam and Mary Walcott confirmed Joseph Ballard's worst fears—Elizabeth was, indeed, under the influence of witchcraft. The girls went on to name the witches who had placed a spell of sickness on his wife. They were Ann Foster; her daughter, Mary Lacey; and Mary's daughter, Mary Lacey Jr. The three accused women were tried, convicted and hanged on Gallows Hill. The list of accused in Andover grew to include men, women and children. Martha Carrier was one of them, and her story is unique.

Martha Carrier was part of the original twenty-three settlers in what is now Andover. Her family was proper and viewed in high standing. As a teenager, Martha took a fancy to a Welch servant her parents employed. His name was Thomas Carrier. Martha soon became pregnant, out of wedlock, with Thomas's child. To soften the blow to her parents and the community, Martha and Thomas were married and moved quickly to Billerica, Massachusetts. Martha's parents were ashamed of her and thought she married below her social status. Her family shunned both her and her husband.

Thomas turned out not to be the average Puritan husband, and Martha was not the average Puritan wife. Thomas was lazy and refused to work. Martha not only took on the responsibilities of cooking, sewing and taking care of the home and children, but she also took over her husband's work, such as bartering for cloth and butter, taking care of the livestock and cutting firewood for the cold winter months. She was outspoken in a time when woman said little or nothing. Martha had five children: three boys, Richard, Andrew and Thomas, and two girls, Sarah and another unnamed girl. The unnamed daughter may have died soon after childbirth, or perhaps she was stillborn.

By 1688, the Carriers were forced to move back to Andover. They lived on the outskirts of the community and depended heavily on their farm for all their needs. Since they were on the outs with their Puritan community, rumors began to fly when people developed smallpox. The Carrier children were barred from public places, as were Martha and Thomas. They seemed to be blamed for just about anything that went wrong in the town. When the witchcraft hysteria claimed Andover, Martha was accused early on by the same girls who accused Ann Foster, Mary Lacey and Mary Lacey Jr. The girls said that the devil had come to them and told them that Martha was promised the title "Queen of the Heb," in lay terms, "Queen of the Hell." Martha apparently stood up to her accusers and called the girls insane for their orchestrated theatrics.

Nevertheless, Martha was carted off to Salem Jail to await her trial. The trial was held on August 2, 1692. All those who were afflicted by Martha's witchcraft paraded forth and gave convincing evidence before the Court of Oyer and Terminer. Many of the witnesses accused Martha of pinching, choking and scratching them. Some accused her of killing their cattle. But what made this

Grave of William Barker, accused of witchcraft. First Burial Ground, North Andover, Massachusetts. *Photo by Bob Abagis.*

story unique was the number of accusations of witchcraft made against Martha. These accusations came from people she never knew as well as her own family. Others who stood accused, like Ann Foster, claimed that Martha had turned them into witches. Ann said in one statement that she had ridden on a broomstick with Martha to Salem Village. When the broomstick broke, Ann grabbed hold of Martha's neck to make the rest of the journey. It was Martha's children who gave the most damning testimony against her. They claimed that she had turned them into witches just like her. Her youngest daughter, Sarah, told the court that her mother brought her the red book of the devil and made her touch it.

Martha never confessed to witchcraft, nor would she implicate any others for the sake of gaining her own freedom. It was the testimony of her children that placed the noose around her neck. Martha was convicted of witchcraft and hanged from Gallows Hill in Salem on August 19, 1692. She is buried at Burying Point Cemetery.

It is said that 80 percent of Andover's total population in 1692 was in some way involved in the witchcraft hysteria. Andover also claims the most confessed witches and the most children arrested for witchcraft.

In the First Burial Ground in North Andover, you will find the graves of some of the accused and their accusers lying in proximity to one another. This cemetery is located on Academy Road.

I have done extensive paranormal research and video examination at this cemetery. I experienced an uneasy feeling and a rush of cold on my arms and legs as I walked in between the graves of the accused and their accusers. My video footage became blurry, which indicates that an energy force was nearby.

There are times in paranormal research when scientific equipment is not needed. You can actually feel the vibrations emitting from the energy source with which you are trying to make contact. I like to say that this is God-given intuition. We all have it. My intuition told me to take a picture right at the spot of the cold rush. I did, and the picture came out completely black, except for a single sky blue translucent orb. An orb is a round or oval form of energy that can often only be seen in a photograph. It is the weakest form of ghost energy and the easiest to capture with your camera.

The spirits that were buried here from the time of the witchcraft hysteria are still in a state of confusion. Through prayer, I tried to make them understand that the world has changed and their views no longer apply. I also read out loud from some of the trial transcripts and talked frankly about the world as it is today. I told them that they need to forgive one another for the acts of the past to be able to move forward into pure spiritual eternity. I believe my healing worked. I took a final walk through the burial ground and passed the places where I had felt the cold rush. All seemed calm. In fact, the entire area was peaceful and serene.

In an article in *Science* magazine in 1976, Linda Caporel suggested that Betty Parris, her playmates and others in Salem at the time of the witchcraft hysteria might have been suffering from a disease called convulsive ergotism. This is caused by ingesting bread or cereal made from rye infected with ergot. Ergot is linked to a fungus that attaches itself to the rye grain before harvest. This usually occurs in humid damp conditions, such as those in the fall of 1691. The grain harvested that fall was used throughout the winter of 1692.

The symptoms of ergotism are violent fits, crawling sensations on the skin, vomiting, choking and hallucinations. The hallucinogenic LSD is a derivative of ergot. Could this have been the cause of the witchcraft hysteria? No one knows for sure.

SLEEP TIGHT

Don't Let the Ghosts Bite

Ever wonder how the phrase "sleep tight" came into usage? Or better yet, the phrase "sleep tight, don't let the bedbugs bite"?
   I once visited the Richard Sparrow Home/Museum in Plymouth, Massachusetts, with my son Bob. This fantastic home dates to the 1640s and is considered to be the oldest home in Plymouth. The guide did a beautiful job of explaining phrases I have heard but of which I never knew the origins. Take, for example, the expression "turning the table." In the mid-1600s, homes were small. Each kitchen item had multiple purposes. The kitchen table was used as a cutting board for freshly killed deer and for preparing meals. Uses for the table were endless. When it came time to sit down and eat, the diners would literally turn the table upside down and eat on the clean side. Hence the saying "turning the tables" was born.
   At one point on our tour, my son Bob and I were led to a bedroom. In the room was a plain and simple bed with a bumpy mattress. In the corners of the bed were solid oak pegs with rope wrapped around them and inserted into a hole. It was explained to us that before going to bed these pegs would have to be turned and then secured in the hole. This would make the bed firm. If the ropes were not tight, the bed and mattress would sag. This is one explanation for the phrase "sleep tight."
   Another explanation has merit as well. It comes from the *Oxford English Dictionary*. According to the OED, "sleep tight" means to

sleep well or soundly. But how can one sleep well or soundly if the bed is sagging and the ropes are not pulled tight? As for the addendum "don't let the bedbugs bite," I think this old phrase speaks for itself.

What constitutes the makeup of a haunted inn or house? Its age, its location or a murder that took place inside its walls? I would have to say yes to all three of these things and a few more. The Merrimack Valley plays host to many inns and old homes. Not all are haunted, but each offers rich history and a wealth of information about lifestyles and growth in the Merrimack Valley. To include all of the haunted inns and houses would require at least two volumes. For the purposes of this book, I have picked out three locations that are accessible on a day trip.

The Rosewood Country Inn

Bradford, New Hampshire

The Rosewood Country Inn in Bradford, New Hampshire, is located along the outer tip of the Merrimack Valley. An easy drive from Manchester, New Hampshire, and surrounding communities, the Rosewood Inn has history, beauty, charm, elegance and, oh yes, ghosts. Built in the early 1850s, the inn was a family home and the property a bustling farm. The Messer family bought the home and farm in the 1890s and turned it into a twenty-two-room inn in 1896. It was called Pleasant View Farm right up until 1956, when the name was changed to the Rosewood Inn.

When it first opened for business in 1896, the inn already had six registered guests. The inn provided bowling, dancing and golf. It also hosted a casino and family activities for its guests. The going rate for all of this fun was only five to seven dollars for the week, including food. There were tents available near a beautiful

The Rosewood Inn, Bradford, New Hampshire. *Photo by Bob Abagis.*

reflecting pond shaded by towering pines for those guests who loved summer camping experiences. The inn itself was an absolutely gorgeous, well-appointed old Victorian home. All of the guests' needs were met in this beautiful New Hampshire inn, a pride of the Merrimack Valley. Year after year, guests returned to the Rosewood Inn. Generations relaxed and enjoyed life as only a summer in New England can provide.

The Rosewood Inn not only enticed average families, but it was also a place for the upper class and movie stars of the era to come and unwind from their hectic schedules. It gave them a chance to see New Hampshire's wild creatures in abundance.

Can you imagine staying in the same room as silent movie icon Charlie Chaplin? What about reading a good book in the room where notable author Jack London stayed? Jack was the first author in American history to actually make a good living from his writing. And girls, when the guys are gathered in the spacious lounge at the

Rosewood Inn, telling manly war stories of their youth, you can get a giggle out of the fact that the spirit of a real swashbuckler is looking down on them. To whom am I referring? None other than Hollywood lady's man Douglas Fairbanks, who was once a guest at the inn. Then there's America's sweetheart Mary Pickford, with her close friends Dorothy and Lillian Gish and Gloria Swanson. Mary started staying at the inn with her family when she was only twelve years old. These megastars of Hollywood's silent screen are long gone, but their spirits still loom large in the rooms at the Rosewood Inn.

I had a pleasant ghostly experience myself at the Rosewood Inn. I was visiting with current innkeepers Dick and Lesley Marquis, who purchased the inn in 1991, as Lesley related a few stories she had heard from their guests. She said that more than a few guests have had ghostly experiences in some of the rooms. All of the rooms in the inn are spectacular—elegant, comfortable and filled with charm. The inn has a welcoming, inviting feel as you enter through the front door, as though you were visiting old friends. Guests have claimed to have been awakened by a ghost sitting on the side of the bed. Some have said that the ghost has tried to get into bed with them. One guest claimed that the ghost made the doll in the bathroom move. Most felt a presence of some kind in the room.

Lesley gave me a tour of the inn, and we stopped in the rooms that guests have reported haunted. She took me to room number seven. I didn't feel anything at first, but when I got closer to the window, I could feel a presence sitting behind me on the bed. The presence kept getting up and going to look out the window and then going back and sitting on the bed. It was what you would call a repetitive motion; in other words, a residual haunting. A residual haunting is a sequence of ghostly motions that repeats itself without any change. It usually occurs where a sudden, tragic incident or death took place. The entity in room number seven was reliving an event in the past.

We moved on to room number twelve. In room number twelve, guests claim to have seen the ghost of a young boy sitting against the wall near the bathroom entrance. My assistant, Bob, took heat readings, and the results were incredible. The meter registered temperatures from sixty-eight to eighty-five degrees in a two-foot-square area. This prompted me to take a few pictures, all of which turned out black. Spirit energy has a way of messing up your pictures. If you ever take a picture in a haunted house and the picture comes out black, this suggests that you have come into contact with an energy force.

From there, we went to room number one. This room is simply delightful. When in the room, I felt a physical change in temperature near the corner window. My first thought was: "Hey, I'm near the window and the temperature can change." I took out the heat meter, and it registered fifty-five to about sixty degrees. I felt my body getting very warm near the window, like I was sweating. I turned toward Lesley and asked her to walk slowly toward the window and to stop when she felt something. Lesley did as I asked, and she, too, felt like the air was warm on her body. There were no heater vents near the window, and we were only measuring the heat in the room.

Another beautifully appointed room was room number nine. Room number nine is called the Mary Pickford room, and I felt the presence of a woman immediately. Her presence was so strong that I took out my dowsing pendulum and started asking questions. I asked if the spirit was a man or a woman, and if it was a woman, I directed it to move the pendulum. To Lesley's surprise, the pendulum started to move. I also asked the spirit if she still had her small white dog with her. The pendulum started to swing wildly. I asked the pendulum to stop, and it did—again, to Lesley's surprise.

To some, this may be a questionable test, but it is supported by the law of inertia. Simply put, the law of inertia says that a mass—in this case, the pendulum—will move at a constant velocity unless affected by an outside force. Objects are lazy and will not simply move (or stop moving) on their own. Some kind of external energy had to move the pendulum to effect the kinds of changes in speed and motion that we witnessed. The pendulum could not have stopped on a dime on its own—this would defy the law of inertia.

After my ghost investigation was complete, I tried to think of what kind of healing I could do for the spirits of the inn. However, not all spirits need healing, and the inn was warm, inviting and, most of all, welcoming. The spirits that dwell there are happy to be there. I wished them a long and happy spirit life. Sometimes it's as simple as that.

If you are interested in a wonderfully romantic time at a fabulous old inn, I highly recommend the Rosewood Inn at 67 Pleasant View Road in Bradford. Visit www.rosewoodcountryinn.com for more information.

The Nashua Red Cross

Nashua, New Hampshire

The Nashua Red Cross is located in a historic home at 28 Concord Street in Nashua, New Hampshire. The Red Cross is very special to my heart, and I want to start this section with a short story about the kindness it bestowed on my son Bob. Some of you may recall the fire that took place in Nashua on February 9, 2009. This fire destroyed an entire building and displaced all of its inhabitants, my son among them.

 I was on my way home from a beautiful wedding at the Mountain Grand View Hotel in the White Mountains. Bob was staying at my house, taking care of the family pets. I got a call from my son on the morning of February 9. He said he went home after caring for the pets and found his entire apartment building on fire. His voice was filled with anxiety. I drove like a maniac toward his apartment, only to find that I wasn't allowed down the street. It was blocked by fire- and policemen. I abandoned my car and ran to the scene, searching for my son. I couldn't find him.

 A Red Cross volunteer approached me and asked if she could help. I said yes and told her I was looking for my son. I was worried that my son had tried to go back into the building to retrieve his belongings. She took his name and checked it against the list of people they had located. To my relief, my son was among those accounted for. A few days after the fire, it was determined that all of the residents, including my son, had lost everything they owned. At this point, the Red Cross came to their aid, providing a credit card of varying amounts to each resident. The card was to help them purchase immediate necessities. The Red Cross also worked with the landlord and others to find them housing. The donations of clothing, food and furniture from the community

The Nashua, New Hampshire Red Cross building. *Photo by CC Carole.*

were overwhelmingly kind. The Red Cross volunteers completely put me and my son at ease with their kindness and generosity. I never knew the scope of unselfish giving that the Red Cross promoted until it struck close to home. I can't thank the organization enough.

I was invited by one of the Red Cross staff members, Karen, to visit the historic home that houses the Nashua Red Cross. She told me bit about the house and the fact that it is haunted. It was built in 1836 and was the home of Barton Carter. Barton's parents named him after Clara Barton, founder of the American Red Cross. Barton did not spend much time in the home. He devoted himself to helping the suffering children of loyalist Spain. He became the administrator of children of the colony at Puigcerda in 1937 for saving the children of Madrid and bringing them there. In his last letter to his parents, he wrote:

> *War is bad enough, but where they take to destruction of innocent people it's just too much. Here they were leading useful happy lives and all of a sudden on a beautiful day they were blown to bits. We have got to end this war soon. I would like to do the most I can do to help. I shall always feel those Puigcerda children are mine. They have already started writing to me as the Padré. Anything to do for Spain, in whatever way, I do for the ideals I believe in and more directly for these Niño's of mine.*

Barton was last seen on April 9, 1938. His family gave his home to the American Red Cross in honor of and to become a memorial to their son.

It is said that in the 1940s Mrs. Pratt, a former board member and the first director of the Nashua Red Cross, lived in the home. She tended to the day-to-day business of the Red Cross and the running of the home as a shelter for people in need. To my understanding, upon Mrs. Pratt's death a wake was held in the front living room of the home. A few of the staff members have felt her presence, and one woman claims to have seen a woman's image at the top of the center staircase. A gentleman seeking refuge at the Red Cross saw a ghostly image of children holding hands skipping around a Christmas tree in the living room.

I led my investigative team through the home. We did not find paranormal activities in each room, but we did find activity in a few rooms. The first was a room on the second floor located at the front of the home past the stairwell. The room was originally used as a nursery and is now a storage closet. My EMF meter kept going off, which is usually an indication of a change in the electromagnetic field in the area. I took a few pictures with my Polaroid instant camera. After the pictures developed, I noticed orbs and other lights called vortex strikes on the pictures. A vortex strike looks like a lightning strike. It is energy of the unearthly type.

We moved deeper into the home to a room with light blue walls. This room was wildly active, but the activity seemed mournful to me. I knew in an instant that this was a room of great sorrow. I took a few pictures in this room, and none came out. It was as if the room did not want the sorrow held within it revealed. I asked Karen about the history of the room with light blue walls. I even said, "I felt great sorrow in that room. What was it used for?" She told me that it was the room where people were given information regarding their loved ones and the tragedies they suffered. The living room, where Mrs. Pratt's wake was held, made my dowsing rods turn in a circle when I asked if there were spirits in the room.

When it came time to perform a healing for the spirits that occupied the home, I sat and thought to myself what would be the best way to glorify them. I say glorify, not heal, because I felt that these spirits were already healed by the loving and comforting assistance the Red Cross had given them in their lives. This is why they are still around us in the home—they are gently saying thank you.

There is ghostly activity in the Red Cross building in Nashua, but it's of the good kind. When you're in Nashua, please do not forget to visit this lovely old home and say hello to the staff volunteers of the Red Cross. Tell them CC said hello! Visit www.nashua.redcross.org for more information.

Winnekenni Castle

Haverhill, Massachusetts

When one thinks of an old home or inn, one usually thinks of a structure that looks somewhat like a house. The home whose history I am about to relate is not typical, not in the least. It started out as the Darling farm overlooking beautiful Kenoza Lake in Haverhill, Massachusetts. *Kenoza* means "Lake of the Pickerel" in the language of the Pentucket Indians, part of the Pennacook Confederation that inhabited the area now called Haverhill. In the year 1873, a home of great magnitude was under construction. It took two years to complete this beautiful specimen. The entire home was made of boulders and rocks from the local area. The boulders and rocks were removed from the surrounding farms to make way for clear fields.

Winnekenni Castle, Haverhill, Massachusetts. *Photo by Bob Abagis.*

Dr. James R. Nichols built his castle home after a visit to Europe. He loved the stone fortresses he saw on his visit abroad and decided to create one for himself on the property he had purchased in 1861. He named it Winnekenni Castle after the Algonquin word meaning "very beautiful." The main purpose of the castle was to serve as a laboratory for the many chemistry experiments he was involved in using agriculture fertilizer. You see, Dr. James R. Nichols was a chemist and agriculturist. He also used the castle as a summer house. Back then, it was said that the view from the castle's rooftop spanned three states, seventeen towns and three counties. One could see the Atlantic Ocean, as well as Mount Argamenticus in the state of Maine. The walls of the castle are four feet thick. In its heyday, it boasted nine bedrooms on the second floor, with one spacious bathroom, or bathing room, as they used to call it. The original library was finished in black walnut. All of the castle's rooms had their own unique style and flair.

In 1885, after a battle with illness, Dr. James R. Nichols sold his home to his cousin, William Webb of Salem, Massachusetts. Webb and his wife loved the opera. They loved it so much that they sponsored Grand Opera singer Geraldine Farrar, a famous star of the opera at the time. Geraldine reigned as queen diva of the Metropolitan Opera for sixteen seasons. She was the highest-paid opera singer of her time. She appeared in 671 performances and held thirty-six parts in 29 operas. To this day, not one opera star can match her record.

The castle stayed in the Webb family for only ten short years. In 1895, it was sold to the City of Haverhill, Massachusetts. A tragic fire destroyed the Victorian-appointed interior in 1969. The Winnekenni Foundation, along with Whittier Regional Technical High School, helped rebuild the castle to its glorious and impressive state once again.

I used to take my children to Winnekenni Castle when they were younger. We would sit on the expansive lawn enjoying picnic lunches in the summer and gazing at the awesome view that surrounded us. The inside of the castle was quite unique; it actually looked and felt like a castle when you walked through it. At times I would get this feeling to look back at the main entrance of the castle. I wasn't the only one to get this feeling. My children had it as well. In fact, one time I asked a couple who were enjoying their lunch on the front lawn why they kept looking back at the main entrance. They told me they felt like they had to. To me, it felt like a pair of eyes was looking at me, and that feeling alone made me turn to look.

I did a bit of digging into the history of Winnekenni Castle and found that a husband and wife were caretakers of the castle from about the 1950s through part of the 1960s. They lived in the carriage house and kept a watchful eye on the people who walked the grounds. Legend has it that they would stare quietly at the passersby, not uttering a sound; they would just stare and nod. This bit of information was the piece of the puzzle I was looking for. I believe the energy from the watchful stare of the former caretakers was the feeling I was getting when enjoying an outing with my children.

I brought along my low-profile equipment to see if there was any activity in and around the castle. I found a surprising amount of ghostly activity registering outside on the grounds rather than inside the castle itself. My EMF meter was in a constant state of blinking when I was outside. When I was inside the castle, the EMF meter didn't go off. This indicated a fluctuation in electrical frequencies. Not trusting my EMF meter, I tried my heat meter. To my surprise, the meter showed varying temperature degrees in and around the outside area I was testing. I was there in June 2009, and the temperature outside was seventy-eight degrees. My meter read temperature from forty-five to eighty-five degrees and all the variables in between. When taking heat readings inside the castle, I found no heat variations to speak of.

Usually when I get fluctuations in temperature of five to ten degrees, I take out my camera and start snapping away. The pictures I took that day were odd. All of the pictures inside the castle appeared normal and clear. Those I took outside the castle that focused on the grounds were normal and clear as well, but when I took a picture of the main entrance, it blurred. I took another picture of the main entrance, and the blur was still there, though it had moved. It was as if the blur was moving across the main entrance door in the picture. Spirit energy, when captured on film, will often blur pictures or make them totally black. The same is the case with video.

The healing techniques I use on the spirits I encounter differ greatly from one spirit to another. In this case, I felt that a healing was needed. I associated the feeling of being stared at with the caretakers' watchful eyes. I also sensed that there was a bit of guilt on the part of the caretakers for not having been there when the fire destroyed the interior. They truly loved their job and this grand old castle. In an effort not to inflame the former caretakers, I crushed up some white sage and sprinkled it near the castle's foundation. I asked the former caretakers' spirits if they wanted a healing performed. I always ask so as not to intrude and do something unwanted by the spirits. In order to work, the healing has to be given in kindness and be welcome.

I started to move in a clockwise manner around the building. I used white sage to clear the air and bring forth positive energy. White sage is used by Native Americans in rituals and also by spiritual people to cleanse their homes. I did not want to light the herb as I do in other healing locations since the castle suffered an enormous tragedy brought on by fire. After I sprinkled white sage around the foundation, I took out my EMF meter. This time, the meter was quiet. My heat meter gave me readings of temperatures within the norm for June. All was calm and peaceful, meaning that my healing was a success.

Feel free to visit the Winnekenni Castle in Haverhill at any time with your own paranormal equipment. I am almost certain that you will find the grounds completely calm and the castle inviting.

Restless Structures

If Walls Could Talk

If walls could talk, we would all be in trouble. Or maybe we would learn something about long-ago times. I hope that the stories in this chapter will offer you a new perspective on places you thought you knew.

Canobie Lake Park and the Dancehall Theatre

When I was in my early teens, I would look forward to those hot sunny days of summer and a trip to Canobie Lake Park in Salem, New Hampshire. Canobie Lake Park was, to me, a wonderland of past energy, present excitement and future plans. I can't recall one person I knew growing up who did not go to and enjoy this fun and memorable amusement park. My neighbor, whom I fondly knew as Grandma Rita, was a coat check girl for the Dancehall Theatre in the park in the 1940s. She had the wildest and most fabulous stories of the stars who performed in the hall and the ghosts that made noises as she worked alone at the end of the evening. For this reason, I had to include a section on the Dancehall Theatre at Canobie Lake Park and dedicate it to Rita. Rita was a kind and beautiful woman, always ready with a laugh and a story, followed by another laugh. A photographer for *LIFE* magazine spotted her and took a picture, and it ended up on the cover of the magazine in the 1940s. She was wearing a leopard print one-piece bathing suit as she sat on the rocks at the beach.

Canobie Lake Park is located at 85 North Policy Road in Salem, on the shores of Canobie Lake. Many of you may not know this, but Canobie was not always the name of the lake. It used to be Policy Lake.

Canobie Lake Amusement Park was created by Hudson, Pelham & Salem (HP&S) Railways in August 1902 as a pleasure resort. After a hard day's work, people would venture to Canobie Lake Park on a trolley and enjoy the refreshing views and delightful breezes of the lake while playing games. The park grounds were beautiful and filled with botanical gardens. Many people dressed in their Sunday best to stroll the fragrant paths with their families. The park hosted an abundance of activities for its social visitors, like canoeing, sporting events, the famous circle swing and, of course, the penny arcade.

Canobie Lake Park was convenient and easy to get to. It was a stop along the newly installed trolley line owned by HP&S Railways. The park grew and prospered during the early years. Salem became a hub of transportation with its trolley and rail services.

On a beautiful Sunday, March 17, 1929, Canobie Lake Park saw its last trolley roll in with visitors. Due to the advent of the automobile, the trolley was no longer needed in the towns that supplied visitors to the park. With the loss of trolley service came the loss of business. Canobie Lake Park closed its gates a short time after trolley service was discontinued.

The closing was short-lived, however. In 1932, the park reopened. One of the main features of the park is the roller coaster the Yankee Cannonball. In 1936, the Yankee Cannonball found its way to the park from Waterbury, Connecticut, and was originally called the Greyhound.

From the 1930s through part of the 1950s, Canobie Lake Park's Dancehall Theatre was the place to go for big city entertainment. In fact, it was so popular that it attracted bands from the big band era like Cab Callaway, Duke Ellington, Jimmy Dorsey, Guy Lombardo, Harry James and Frank Sinatra. As the years passed from the '50s to the present day, the bands changed to the likes of the Beach Boys, Gene Pitney, Sonny and Cher and Aerosmith. The energy and electricity from those awesome acts can still be felt as you walk into the Dancehall Theatre. As you enter the hall, you can actually feel a rush of excitement. I believe this rush is energy from the past. Grandma Rita told me that she would get this same rush every time she went to work and especially when she was there alone at night.

It was misting outside on the evening I visited the hall. The park closed a short time after I arrived due to the inclement weather. From the exterior of the Dancehall Theatre, one could only imagine the history within its walls. Once inside the hall, I asked that the lights be dimmed but not turned off because I wanted to see any shadows that might appear. Then I asked to be left alone with my assistant. I always bring another person with me on an investigation, for my own safety. I started the investigation in the main hall and from there moved on to investigate the dressing rooms.

The main hall literally takes you back in time. Just the presence of the stage conjures up visions of lives long past. As I was facing the stage, I closed my eyes and listened intently. Maybe it was my imagination, but I actually could hear toe tapping and several swooshes on the stage in front of me. It almost sounded rhythmic. I opened my eyes and there was nothing there. As a professional ghost hunter and clairvoyant, I know exactly what I heard—the sounds of energy from the past.

When I hear things like this on an investigation, I always take out my camera and start taking pictures. I am looking for orbs and ecto masses. Ecto masses are foglike shapes captured on camera. Sometimes you can actually see ecto masses with the naked eye, but don't confuse them with low-lying fog. It is easy to tell the difference between the two: fog usually remains in the same location for a period of time and slowly dissipates, while ecto masses are there one minute and gone the next.

Taking pictures turned out to be a good idea. I captured orbs and a huge ecto mass right in the middle of the stage, where the sounds had originated. Moving on to the dressing rooms, I noticed something out of the corner of my eye. When I turned to see what

Gene Pitney with Stephanie Micklon. Notice the floating ecto mass. *Photo courtesy of Stephanie Micklon.*

it was, there was nothing there. This is usually the way you see spirit energy—a fleeting glimpse in your peripheral vision.

The dressing room looked like any entertainer's dressing room. The photo of famous entertainer Gene Pitney with Stephanie Micklon was taken inside this very dressing room. In the picture, you can clearly see an ecto mass swirling around and engulfing Gene and Stephanie. In the picture of Cher from 1965, orbs float around the singer onstage. I started to take heat measurements and quickly found that the levels were fluctuating, indicating the presence of an

Cher onstage at the Dancehall Theatre. Notice the orbs around her. *Photo courtesy of Stephanie Micklon.*

entity. In fact, the room had a heavy feel to it. When I reached the middle of the stage, my meter turned off on its own and my camera batteries died. Even my backup camera would not work properly.

With my equipment failing, I decided to do a quick healing before something else happened and I was forced to leave. I positioned myself at center stage and recited the following words: "Thank you for your dreams." Entertainers take their dreams of pleasing us to the ultimate level. I was recognizing these past performers for the decades of love and dreams that they put in our hearts. The Canobie Lake Park Dancehall Theatre is alive and well and will continue to share the dreams of its entertainers with us for many years to come. Next time you take a trip to the park, walk over to the Dancehall Theatre, pop your head inside and feel the rush.

Tewksbury State Hospital

Among the many professions I decided to try while searching for what I wanted to be when I grew up was auxiliary police officer for the City of Lawrence, Massachusetts. I received my training at North East Regional Police Institute (NERPI) on the grounds of the Tewksbury Hospital in Tewksbury, Massachusetts.

Tewksbury Hospital was built in 1852 and was originally called Tewksbury Almshouse. *Almshouse* is defined in *Webster's New World Dictionary* as "a home for people too poor to support themselves; poorhouse." Poorhouses date back to the fourteenth century, when

Tewksbury State Hospital. *Photo by CC Carole.*

the elderly were housed and cared for. These almshouses were often privately financed by the city and towns that used them. The Tewksbury Almshouse was the first of its kind, being financed by the Commonwealth of Massachusetts. It opened its doors to the indigent, with beds for about 500, on May 1, 1854. By December 2, 1854, the number of poor under its roof had grown to 2,193 people. At that time, the almshouse had only fourteen employees.

In 1866, Tewksbury Almshouse became the first poorhouse to house the insane. While delving into the history of the almshouse, I found an interesting fact. The standard breakdown of the facility, as of 1874, was 40 percent of the rooms used for the insane ward, 27 percent for a hospital and 33 percent for caring for the elderly poor.

As time went on, the need for nurses to work and care for the patients of the Tewksbury Almshouse grew. Understanding the unique situation of the nurses and their pledge to care for the poor, Tewksbury Almshouse instituted a Home Training School for Nurses in 1870. By 1894, it had its own fully equipped three-year program for nursing.

The almshouse changed throughout the years and redesigned itself to better fit the needs of the people it served. In 1900, the facility was called Tewksbury State Hospital. In 1909, the name changed to Massachusetts State Infirmary, and in 1938, it became the Tewksbury State Hospital and Infirmary. Today, it is known as Tewksbury Hospital. What it will be tomorrow, no one knows.

A famous person once lived within the walls of the Tewksbury Almshouse. Annie Sullivan was a resident there for four years, from 1876 to 1880. At age twenty, she became the live-in tutor and governess to Helen Keller. Helen Keller was a blind and deaf woman who achieved enormous popularity for overcoming obstacles thrust upon her by a childhood illness. Keller was the first blind student of her time to graduate from Radcliffe University with a bachelor of arts degree. She was also a champion of women's suffrage. Annie Sullivan taught Helen by using the sign language alphabet, writing in the palm of the girl's hand. This system of sign language was developed by Spanish monks during medieval times and is used by sign language experts around the world today.

Tewksbury Hospital, despite all of the good it has done for the poor and the insane, has had its share of trouble. This trouble was monumental and extremely detrimental to the hospital, community and patients who lived there. On Thursday, March 22, 1883, Governor Benjamin Franklin Butler of Lowell, Massachusetts, launched an investigation into charges of patient abuse at Tewksbury Hospital. He was known for waging war against charitable organizations. None of the charges were found to be criminal, no one was prosecuted and no legislation was brought against the hospital, but after a review of the facts in the case, not one person who was born or lived in Tewksbury was allowed to speak of what they knew regarding the allegations brought forth by Butler.

The following are excerpts from the *Lowell Sun Weekly* of 1883. (If you would like to read the articles in depth, visit www.tewksburyhistoricalsociety.org/Archives/index.html, scroll down to the featured items and click on *Lowell Sun Weekly*, 1883).

> *Gov. Butler's Charges Against the Tewksbury Almshouse Management, March 22, 1883*
> *His Excellency the Governor, and in the veto message of the appropriation bill, being substantial, that there is gross extravagance and management of the Tewksbury almshouse; that 70 percent of the appropriation, substantially, used for salaries; and that there have been found 150 to 250 bodies of babies sold to medical institutions a year. The committee decided to hear the Governor's evidence of these points as the basis of procedure.*
>
> *Dr. John Dixwell, of Boston was the first witness called by Gov. Butler. He testified that he was a regular physician, living at No. 6 Pemberton square: that he was educated at Harvard college, and that he graduated from the medical school in 1873. He testified that during the three years he saw and knew of several hundred bodies of infants, each year, being brought to the school for dissection. They were brought there in trunks, in a country team, and were deposited in a little anteroom in crates on shelves until the students were ready to use them. The students obtained the bodies by applying Bill Andrews, now dead, who fixed the price at from $3 to $5 each, for infants or for part of an adult, according to the supply. Andrews was a prize fighter; he died by suicide. The bodies of the infants were sought for by persons who wished to practice dissection, because they could easily be taken in a bundle and carried home. Personally he had two or three every week, during the season. Some of those dissected showed that they had died of starvation.*

The witness said that Andrews told him the bodies came from the Tewksbury almshouse. Dr. Dixwell said that he had given substantially the same evidence before the grand jury for Suffolk county about five years ago. Have seen remains of infants packed up for disposal with those of animals, birds, ect.

I ventured to the Tewksbury Hospital to explore and investigate these rumors and also those that I heard while attending the police academy and working at the hospital as a nursing assistant.

The hospital grounds are absolutely gorgeous and well maintained. The buildings are old, as I remembered them. As I started to walk around and get reacquainted with my surroundings, I became anxious. It was the same anxiety I used to feel when I parked my car and started heading to the academy or to work. My past experiences at Tewksbury Hospital were quite odd. It wasn't until I began the historical research for this book that all of the pieces of those experiences fell into place.

While attending the police academy, I would see shadows moving across the empty halls and entering rooms. At first, I would ask if anyone else saw the shadows. The response was always: it's just the ghost that lives here. The ghost didn't make any noise, but it was still eerie to witness.

My experience working at the hospital was a little different. As a nursing assistant, I would walk through the interconnecting hallways, running errands and delivering items to the patients. I always had the feeling that I would get lost in the enormous structures that make up the Tewksbury Hospital. What bothered me the most were the sounds I heard. It was always the same thing—the sound of a woman weeping. I tried to tell myself that the sound came from a patient, but there were no patients in the areas where I heard the weeping. I now believe that the weeping was residual energy from the staff or nurses who cared for the poor or from the women who lost their children to starvation and infant diseases.

I tried to shake off the anxious feeling, but it persisted even as I walked through the front doors of the hospital. In an effort to not call too much attention to myself, I walked to the visitor's waiting room and sat down. After I regained my bearings, I headed directly down a long hallway, which eventually led to another passage. This passage led to a tunnel that connected some of the buildings. It appeared that the tunnels were no longer in use. I stood where the tunnel entrance used to be and started to take out my dowsing pendulum to ask the spirits if they wanted a healing. At that moment, I felt a hand tapping my upper arm near my shoulder, as if in recognition and approval of my presence and impending healing.

As a Usui Reiki master and Karuna Reiki physician, I knew that this type of healing was exactly what the hospital needed. Reiki is an ancient and sacred Japanese healing art. Reiki healers place their hands on or just above the person they are healing. Energy flows into and through the practitioner and into the patient to provide healing. When performing Reiki, one's hands heat up as the energy is passed from the practitioner to the patient. Reiki can also be performed to heal the past, present and future. I knew that I needed to heal the ill will of the past that flowed into the present and would be carried into the future. For this, I used Karuna Reiki. Karuna Reiki is fast, strong and accurate. Karuna Reiki and Usui Reiki complement each other. Karuna Reiki works faster, and I felt that speed was of the essence. For me, Reiki is a private healing that I do in silence.

When I finished the healing, the anxious feeling left me. As I walked back through the building to the parking lot, all seemed well. The air was tranquil and calm. Whether the weeping will stop, I can't say for certain. Even when a healing is performed, spirits—like humans—may still feel loss and continue to mourn.

I am a certified teacher in the art of Reiki, and if you would like to learn this beautiful art, contact me at ccthehuntress@yahoo.com.

Table for Two

Room for One More?

When I go to a restaurant to relax and have a good dinner, I like spirits to be in the form of a fine wine. But in my line of work, spirits often mean an unexpected guest at the table.

I have been to many so-called haunted restaurants and have marveled at the rumored stories that surround and enchant the dining guests. They can almost make one a bit scared to take a trip to the restroom alone! I chose to include the restaurants in this chapter not so much for their haunted reputations but because of their rich histories, which fuel the ghostly tales.

The Country Tavern

Nashua, New Hampshire

The Country Tavern, located at 452 Amherst Street in Nashua, New Hampshire, is a quaint antique Cape home that houses an

The Country Tavern, Nashua, New Hampshire. *Photo by Bob Abagis.*

up-to-date gourmet restaurant. The food is incredible, and the prices are pretty great too. The property was originally the Leach farm for over two hundred years. The actual street address was not designated until 1964. Until then, it was simply called the House on Amherst Road.

The house was built in 1741, and from 1798 to 1980 it remained a family residence. It is said that the ghost that haunts the Country Tavern is a woman named Elizabeth Ford. (For the record, her name was Lizzy Leach Rollins Ford, but because so many people refer to her as Elizabeth, so will I.) As the legend goes, Elizabeth was the young wife of a jealous sea captain. Her husband left on a journey out to sea, and upon his return, he found that his wife had given birth to a baby boy. Adding the months of his absence, the captain realized that the baby could not possibly be his. He murdered his wife, threw her body down the well and buried the infant boy under a tree in the backyard.

Historical evidence supports some of the story surrounding Elizabeth and her sea captain husband. On October 26, 1673, a two-hundred-square-mile tract of land was chartered to Massachusetts to form a new township. This area, which ran from Chelmsford, Massachusetts, all the way north to the Lakes Region, was named Dunstable, after the English hometown of one of the founding families. Nashua was settled in the late 1700s by migrants from Chelmsford. Chelmsford was known as a retirement destination for sea captains.

Elizabeth's aunt, Mary Leach Rollins, adopted Elizabeth in November 1868 from her nephew, John, and his wife, Fanny. John and Fanny Leach went on to have several other children after Elizabeth's adoption. So why did John and Fanny let Mary adopt their firstborn child? One reason could be that Mary Leach Rollins never had any children of her own. Another could be that John and Fanny were poor, and Mary stepped in to legally care for the child.

Elizabeth was born severely mentally handicapped. In fact, after Mary's death in 1887, Elizabeth married her legal guardian, Fred Ford—a much older man. Fred Ford placed Elizabeth in a home for the mentally insane in Maine shortly after their marriage. Was Fred Ford a sea captain? He is listed in the town census as a traveler. Perhaps he was a seaworthy traveler. There is no evidence to support that a baby boy was born to Elizabeth. However, the Leach farm was a great distance from the center of Nashua, and things could have happened there that were not reported.

My encounter with the ghost of Elizabeth took place in the women's restroom. Well aware of the rumors and stories about Elizabeth, I decided to take an extended visit to the restroom and turn off the light. I snapped a few digital pictures, and lo and behold, I captured orbs in every picture. When I tried to turn on the light, I couldn't find the light switch. I decided to open the door to let in some light from the hallway. The door wouldn't open. I pulled and pulled, but it appeared to be stuck, as though it had been nailed shut. The air seemed to get heavy, making it almost humid in the restroom. I know spirits and the tricks they use to scare us, so I asked Elizabeth to stop playing games and open the door. I tried the door again and it opened. It seems that all Elizabeth wanted was to have her existence validated. Sometimes healing can be effected through a frank conversation that acknowledges the spirit's presence.

If you are ever in Nashua, consider having a meal at the Country Tavern at 452 Amherst Street and saying hello to its very friendly spirit, Elizabeth.

Hannah Jack's/The Common Man Restaurant

Merrimack, New Hampshire

I remember a lovely and exciting haunted restaurant called Hannah Jack's (1970–2005). It is now the Common Man Restaurant at 304 Daniel Webster Highway in Merrimack, New Hampshire, though it is sometimes still referred to by its former name. I often wonder where it got its name and the history behind the beautifully restored historical restaurant.

As I researched the restaurant, I came across an amazing amount of information regarding a very famous person—Dr. Matthew Thornton. Dr. Thornton was one of the original signers of the Declaration of Independence. His grave is located directly across the street from the restaurant. His story is entwined with the rich history of the astounding woman who became the namesake of the tavern and, later, restaurant.

Hannah Jack was born in 1742. Her family settled in Chester, New Hampshire, sometime before 1747. Andrew Jack, her father, was a Presbyterian. He was listed in the census as being employed as a warden. Her mother, Mary Morrison, was listed as wife. They were originally of Scottish descent, moved to Ireland and then came to America, settling in Londonderry, New Hampshire, and then Chester. Hannah married Dr. Matthew Thornton at the age of eighteen. Matthew was forty-four years old, and this was the first marriage for them both. Hannah and Matthew had five children, four of whom survived into adulthood. Their names were Andrew, James, Matthew, Mary and Hannah.

The Common Man Restaurant, formerly Hannah Jack's, Merrimack, New Hampshire. *Photo by CC Carole.*

The restaurant property and structure were first owned by Edward Goldstone Lutwyche. Mr. Lutwyche was known to be a Tory, and his property was seized by the Continental Congress. Hannah's husband bought the seized property in 1780. In the early 1800s, Dr. Thornton's son James turned the home into a tavern. He named the tavern after his mother. Many political and war stories were shared within the walls of Hannah Jack's Tavern. The home and the cemetery across the street were listed on the National Register of Historic Places in 1978.

Hannah died on December 5, 1786, and was followed by her husband on June 24, 1803. Both are buried at the Matthew Thornton Cemetery across the street. No wonder the place is haunted—the graves are so close to the house turned tavern that they loved!

The ghosts that are rumored to be haunting the Common Man vary. Staff members say that there is the spirit of an Indian in the basement. There are also rumors of a man walking around in old clothes. Some say that James, Hannah and Matthew's son, hanged himself from the doorjamb of the one hundred room. Others say that there is a connection to the Underground Railroad and that the tunnel enters the restaurant from the right side of the basement and empties into the woods before the Merrimack River.

I headed to the Common Man Restaurant at about three thirty in the afternoon. The restaurant actually opens a bit later for dinner. I recognized the general manager, Jim Peritti, from all of the times I've enjoyed a meal there with my family. I asked him to show me the basement. I was looking for the breach in the wall that was used as an entrance to the house by travelers on the Underground Railroad. After searching the granite foundation for breaches, I noticed light coming from an area on the other side of a granite wall. In one end of this area there was a walled-off storage section. Past the storage area, on the other side of that wall, was the rest of the basement. The area was not visible from the main basement, and there was no access point. In other words, you couldn't get to it.

I climbed up on a high stool and peered over the wall. Through spider webs and dust, I saw exactly what I hoped to see—a breach of sorts in the granite wall. I believe I found the entrance to the tunnel that the slaves used on their journey to freedom.

I returned to the front stairs. Jim had received a call and left me by myself. The upstairs bar was empty, and no employees had arrived yet. I was startled by a woman dressed in a long grayish blue dress at the top of the stairs. She had on a white apron over her dress, and wore a small bonnet on her head. Her gray hair was pulled up under the bonnet. She was holding a folded cloth over her arm. She had a slight smile on her face and looked content. I looked straight at her, and she at me, and then she smiled, turned and disappeared. She was not translucent but vivid and solid looking.

I remembered reading that a local ghost investigation group from the Nashua area had investigated the Common Man. One of the female investigators reported seeing what I saw: a woman dressed in the long gray dress of another time period. The investigators decided it was probably a residual haunting because the ghostly figure did not react to the investigator. But residual hauntings do not smile at you. That one gesture was a dead giveaway to me. I believe that the woman I saw was an employee of the original Hannah Jack's tavern, based on her dress, bonnet and folded cloth. The smile she gave me suggests that I was welcome there.

I thought of an appropriate healing. I validated her existence by thanking her for greeting me so kindly and making me feel at home in the tavern. I also told her that I liked the food she cooked.

People were starting to arrive for dinner, and I was hungry as well. I sat down to enjoy a meal, and my waitress greeted me with a smile. I knew in that moment that I had not only connected with the ghost but also healed her by thanking her for a job well done.

Tortilla Flats

Merrimack, New Hampshire

A renowned restaurant in the Merrimack Valley is Tortilla Flats, located at 595–597 Daniel Webster Highway in Merrimack, New Hampshire. If you like Mexican food, it can't be beat. When I was younger, I knew that the Flats, as we call it, was haunted, but I didn't know by what. During my research, I discovered who the ghosts are and which parts of the restaurant they like to haunt the most.

Tortilla Flats comprises two homes joined together. The house I am most interested in is the older home, at 597 Daniel Webster Highway, which was built in 1776. The land used to reach about a quarter mile back to the Merrimack River. To understand the significance of the home, one must first understand a bit about the history of the town of Merrimack.

Sometime after 1606, King James I of England formed a committee consisting of forty noblemen, knights and gentlemen called "the council established at Plymouth, England, in America." This patent, or charter, was the foundation of all grants made by the king(s) of England to the country of New England. The area in which Merrimack is situated was originally part of a king's grant. The land stretched

Tortilla Flats, Merrimack, New Hampshire. Notice the huge orb in front of the restaurant. *Photo by CC.Carole.*

all the way from Chelmsford, Massachusetts, to the Lakes Region of New Hampshire. It encompassed roughly two hundred square miles. As time passed, it was eventually broken into towns and then into the two states of Massachusetts and New Hampshire.

The slave trade and the Underground Railroad existed in many towns in New Hampshire, and Merrimack was one of them. Tortilla Flats is rumored to have been a safe house. The house changed owners more than twenty-one times, and the current owner is Powell Reality. Tortilla Flats has been serving excellent Mexican food for over thirty years and is still going strong. Also going strong are rumors of the ghosts that haunt the restaurant. The following are some rumors and facts about the ghosts of Tortilla Flats:

RUMOR: A man named Zechariah was murdered in the front room.
FACT: Zechariah was the name of a previous owner. There is no record of a murder, but patrons have seen a ghostly shadow out

of the corner of their eyes when in or near the front room. The waitstaff and kitchen staff have seen the ghost of a woman and little girl near the back of the house.

RUMOR: Tortilla Flats was a stop on the Underground Railroad.
FACT: I discovered a breach in the wall in the original basement that indicated where the tunnel came into the house, confirming that the home was a safe house. I believe that the ghost of the little girl is a slave child looking for food. The ghost of the woman could be a female slave who passed through the house on the Underground Railroad.

I held an event at Tortilla Flats, during which I presented the building's history and the rumors of its ghosts. I offered a mini paranormal class and invited guest speakers to inform the group about paranormal oddities. Then we went on a full-fledged ghost hunt.

Not everyone can afford ghost equipment, so I asked the patrons to bring from home wire coat hangers to use as dowsing rods. Dowsing rods have been used for thousands of years to detect energy fluctuations. The homemade dowsing rods spun like crazy. Lots of people captured orbs on camera. Everyone had a good time, and they were amazed by the way they, too, could communicate with spirits. I did not feel that a healing was necessary. The spirits at Tortilla Flats seem happy and comfortable, especially when people are there to validate their existence.

HAUNTED MILLS AND MORE

Terror in Textiles

My parents, Mary and Glenn, grew up in Pawtucket, Rhode Island. So did my grandparents Mary and Joseph. They lived two blocks from the nation's largest silk mill, owned by Joseph Otts, and raised their family there. My grandfather's sister, Jenny, worked at the silk mill. Both my grandmother and grandfather worked in a Lyon Fabrics mill, part of the Blackstone Valley in Central Falls, Rhode Island, a short walk from Pawtucket. I say a short walk because my grandparents used to walk to work every day.

My grandfather was a smash and loom fixer in the mill. His job was to untangle the thread that became tangled as it passed through the weaving loom. He was also in charge of keeping the weaving loom in working order. My grandmother was a spooler. She put the different colored threads into the weaving loom, one thread at a time, to create beautifully patterned materials that were then shipped to factories, where they were cut into patterns to make clothes. My uncle Steven was a pattern cutter for one of the mills where my grandmother shipped material. It was located right across the street from the mill where my grandparents worked.

My mother also worked in a few different mills in Central Falls to help put my father through Providence College. My aunt Sally, my mother's sister, married Eddy, whose father owned a mill that made strapping. And then there was my father's father, my grandfather Albert, who also worked in a Pawtucket steel mill for

The mills on Canal Street in Lawrence, Massachusetts. *Photo by CC Carole.*

years. With all of this family history, I couldn't wait to start writing this particular chapter. Even though my family is from Pawtucket and not the Merrimack Valley, the importance of Pawtucket must be established before I can write another word regarding mills.

In 1793, a gentleman named Samuel Slater built the first water-powered textile mill in Pawtucket. The Slater Mill began the American Industrial Revolution. Samuel Slater is known as the father of the Industrial Revolution in the United States. The Slater Mill complex was a series of buildings that looked more like houses than a typical brick mill. Each building had its own special purpose in the manufacturing of cloth. One of the buildings would be used for water-powered spinning of raw cotton into yarn. After the yarn was created, it was moved to another building, or sometimes a worker's home, to be woven into cloth. Mr. Slater also created the model of a mill village, which employed entire families and paid them with credit. This credit was used at mill-owned stores. This way, production would increase at a rapid pace with the added cash flow. Slater's mill villages included houses, churches, schools and recreation for its employees. One place of pride was the Slatersville mill village in North Smithfield, Rhode Island.

New Hampshire and Massachusetts have rich textile mill histories, and Samuel Slater was an intricate part of them. His Rhode Island system of water-powered mills was of primary use in the mills of the Merrimack Valley.

The cotton Boott Mill in Lowell, Massachusetts, was named after Kirk Boott, one of Lowell's early industrialists. In 1830, the Boott Mill was constructed and would soon become one of the nation's largest inventive designs of its time. It took its design from the Waltham mill and incorporated it on a much larger and more efficient scale. The design of the Waltham mill is extremely important to note because it was the first to house the entire manufacturing process of cloth in one vertical building. The Boott Mill, like the Slater Mill, had a mill village of enormous proportions that catered to its employees with churches, schools and shops.

These mill complexes were in themselves working cities, with all the conveniences and necessities that an employee's family could want and need. This kept the workforce solid and production increasing. When an accident occurred, there was no compensation for the injured and no punishment for those who caused it. Accidents were commonplace in the mills because the working areas were poorly lit, the hours were long and most of the work was done by women and children. This was a recipe for disaster, as you will soon find out.

The Pemberton Mill

Lawrence, Massachusetts

The Pemberton Mill in Lawrence, Massachusetts, was built in 1853. Its engineer was Charles Bigelow. The project to build the mill was financed by John Lowell and his brother-in-law, J. Pickering Putnam, at a staggering cost of $850,000. Lowell and Putnam sold the mill in 1857 to George Howe and David Nevins Sr. for $500,000, leaving Lowell and Putnam with a $350,000 loss.

The Pemberton Mill produced cloth and was best known for its production of flannel. It was five stories high and 280 feet long, with a width of 84 feet. Given its enormous size, its new owners decided to increase its productivity by adding more equipment and employees to the upper floors. For a time, this worked, with profits exceeding $1,500,000 dollars annually. The mill also had twenty-seven hundred spindles—wooden spikelike sticks at one end with a circular whorl (spiral pattern) used to spin wool, cotton and different fibers into thread. It also housed seven hundred looms. A loom is a machine that takes the thread and weaves it together to create textiles.

Little did Nevins and Howe know, but the Pemberton Mill had been built in haste with deplorable workmanship. The walls and support beams had to be reinforced. The sheer weight being placed on the floors and walls was well beyond the acceptable allowance for a building of such proportions. The concrete mortar was substandard and started to crack, allowing the bricks to give way. What happened next constitutes Massachusetts's worst textile industrial accident to date.

On January 10, 1860, the Pemberton Mill collapsed with six hundred employees inside. The following are a few excerpts from the January 11, 1860 *New York Times*:

> *Lawrence, Mass., Tuesday, Jan. 10—9 P.M.*
> *One of the most terrible catastrophes on record occurred in the city this afternoon. The Pemberton Mill fell with a sudden crash about 5 o'clock while some six or seven hundred operatives were at work.*
>
> *The mills are a complete wreck. Some two to three hundred persons are supposed to be still in the ruins.*
>
> *Every few minutes some poor wretch is dragged from his or her prison, and it is heartrending to hear their cries as they are drawn out with legs and arms crushed and torn. One man shockingly mangled and partly under the bricks, deliberately cut his own throat to end his agony.*

City Hall, Lawrence, Massachusetts, was used as a hospital and morgue following the collapse of the Pemberton Mill. *Photo by CC Carole*.

The whole city seems in mourning. Many are running through the streets and with frantic cries searching the ruins.

The Ruins in Flames, 12o'Clock-MIDNIGHT
Calamity succeeds calamity! In ten minutes the whole mass of ruins has become one sheet of flames. The screams and moanings of the poor buried creatures can be distinctly heard, but no power can save them.

Lawrence City Hall was used as a makeshift hospital and morgue. Surgeons and nurses came from distant towns and states to help the victims of the collapse. Lawrence lost over two hundred people in the collapse of the Pemberton Mill, and hundreds of others were injured, not to mention the mental toll taken on an entire city struggling with grief.

In the aftermath, it was concluded that the Pemberton Mill was poorly constructed and that Charles Bigelow, head engineer, had been well aware of the mill's serious construction defects. Bigelow was brought to court for his part in the collapse but was found not guilty. As was the case in most mill accidents, no one was punished. The workers suffered the most, receiving no compensation for their losses. The unrecognized dead from the Pemberton Mill disaster are honored with a monument placed in the Bellevue Cemetery in Lawrence. The monument reads: "In Memory of the Unrecognized Dead Who Were Killed by the Fall of the Pemberton Mill, Jan. 10, 1860."

I have said many times that at the highest point of impact—or when and where the tragedy took place—can be found the most paranormal energy. I visited the site of the original Pemberton Mill. On the site is another mill that was built shortly after the original one collapsed. As I gazed at the mill, I couldn't help but think of the night of the mill disaster. I honestly believe I could still hear the cries and moans of the workers who were trapped inside. As for scientific results, I decided not to proceed with any testing. I didn't need to. In fact, if you travel to the site of the mill today, you will feel the energy of the past.

I am a healer, and these spirits needed to be healed. They were screaming for comfort and release from the burning sensation they were still experiencing. I called loudly to the spirits in front of me,

The Pemberton Mill Monument at Bellevue Cemetery, Lawrence, Massachusetts. *Photo by CC Carole.*

and with a thoughtful prayer of release, I gave them the power to go to a place of comfort and freedom. Where they go from there is based on their personal belief systems, not mine. The wind started to blow very hard, and when it stopped, so did the screams and moans. All was peaceful and calm.

The Abbott-Downing Company and the Concord Coach

Concord, New Hampshire

The Merrimack Valley was home to many textile mills. But did you know that it was also home to a very unique product manufactured in Concord, New Hampshire? This product was the main ingredient of the transportation industry around the world. It also starred in many Wild West movies. It is none other than the Concord Coach, manufactured by the Abbott-Downing Company. While researching this book, I was filled with pride knowing that Concord, part of the Merrimack Valley, had left its mark worldwide in such an incredible way.

The Abbott-Downing Company was formed in 1826 by Stephen Abbott and Lewis Downing. They were in the business of making wagons and other horse-drawn transportation. The horse-drawn coaches, wagons and carriages they manufactured were purchased by businesses and individuals around the world. In fact, here in the Merrimack Valley, there probably isn't a road that an Abbott-Downing horse-drawn wagon didn't venture down. The energy of the past from these magnificent carriages, and the animals that pulled them, still remains. For this reason, I pursued a paranormal investigation of the Abbott-Downing Company.

The horse-drawn vehicles manufactured by the Abbott-Downing Company filled many voids in the ever expanding Merrimack Valley.

Doctors would purchase a specially equipped wagon or carriage to make house calls. This vehicle had compartments for supplies and a comfortable seat for the doctor on his long trips into the wilderness to see patients. Not all people lived in the city; many lived in remote wilderness locations. The Abbott-Downing Company was well aware of this fact and manufactured a state-of-the-art vehicle that was durable and lightweight. Being lightweight, it was easier on the horses that pulled it.

By the time Abbott and Downing disbanded their partnership, more than seven hundred Concord Coaches had been sold. That number does not include the wagons and carriages that had been purchased over the twenty-one-year partnership.

The most popular of all the vehicles was the Concord Coach. This coach was used on mail lines in the United States. Many stage lines used the coach for its versatility and comfort. Australia, Canada, South America, South Africa and the United Kingdom all enjoyed the benefits of the Concord Coach. The Abbott-Downing Company had a winning design. While other companies made improvements on their original designs and tried to make the coach as comfortable and rugged as the Concord, they couldn't quite hit the mark. The original design of the Concord Coach was literally left unchanged because it was perfect from the start. Why mess with the best?

The secret to the Concord Coach's success was its springless suspension. Strapping was used instead. Most designs of the day included a series of springs to buffer the bounce and stabilize the rough ride for a passenger inside the carrying compartment. The ride was even rougher and more unstable for the driver at the front of the coach. I recently had the opportunity to drive a team of horses in a carriage with strapping suspension instead of spring. It was not an Abbott-Downing product, but the suspension was similar. My drive was a complete joy and my bottom didn't hurt a bit!

The wide strapping that Abbott-Downing used ran lengthwise under the coach. This created a swinging feeling that was very comfortable. The strapping was made of durable bull hide, which had its own natural give in the elements. The interior of the coach was exquisite. Custom leather seats, a brightly hand-painted exterior and curtains made from cloth manufactured in the mills of the Merrimack Valley set the Concord Coach apart from other carriages. The body of the coach was made of strong oak and the wheels of ash. Instead of a hard wood that would crack and break under stressful road conditions, softer wood, like ash, tended to be forgiving on the rough-surfaced roads. Mark Twain called the Concord Coach "an imposing cradle on wheels."

San Francisco's Louis McLane, president of the Pioneer State Company of California, purchased a Concord Coach. This is how the magnificent Concord Coach made its way to California. One was also purchased by Colonel William F. "Buffalo Bill" Cody after he used it in his Wild West show. Bill Cody outran the Indians and raiders in his youth on the historic Pony Express. He also was a noted scout, bringing people west to California to seek their fortunes and a new life. In later years, he was an entertainer and showman in the Wild West show that toured the globe.

A coach very similar to the one Buffalo Bill used in his famous show carried the mail on the infamous Deadwood mail line. This was a mail route from Cheyenne to Deadwood via Laramie, Wyoming. This area of our nation was filled with ruthless banditti of the plains. Banditti are lawless criminals who live by plundering. The Deadwood mail line was considered the most dangerous and deadliest line in the developing United States.

In 1876, Martha Canary was a passenger, along with six men, on the Deadwood stage line. They were riding in a Concord Coach from Deadwood to Wild Birch, part of the Black Hills. The coach was attacked, and the driver of the six-horse team was shot with an arrow and killed. While arrows and bullets flew wildly, Martha climbed into the driver's seat, gathered the reins—or ribbons, as they were called—in her hands and started to whip the team. She singlehandedly brought the coach and its passengers to safety. The six men sat paralyzed in their seats, afraid to move. Martha made great time and arrived at Wild Birch with the men too embarrassed to speak. This courageous woman was fondly known in the history books of the West as "Calamity Jane." Calamity Jane was a western scout under Buffalo Bill and is buried near "Wild Bill" Hickok in Deadwood, South Dakota.

On July 4, 1895, Concord received a visitor like no other. Buffalo Bill Cody arrived and brought with him his original coach, built in 1863. Buffalo Bill entertained an audience of over twenty thousand people with one of his famous Wild West shows. People came from states away to get a look at the famous cowboy. They were amazed at the

Concord Coach #13, used for the Centre Harbor–North Conway route to the White Mountains. *Photo by CC Carole.*

way he could ride and re-create the tales of the Old West in the arena. His acts consisted of riding for the Pony Express to Indian battles and showing off his skills of marksmanship. But the star attraction, besides Bill, was always his timeless Concord Coach.

In my youth, I used to ride a beautiful quarter horse named Coco. We would travel all over Chelmsford, Massachusetts, and surrounding towns, investigating old trails and blazing a few new ones. There is one trail I remember well. It was an old stagecoach trail that went from Boston to Lowell, situated on the corner of Billerica and Turnpike Roads in Chelmsford. I remember riding all the way down to Billerica and back again in the same day with a few friends. We could still see the deep ruts in the old road made by the stagecoaches and wagons that traveled the path, delivering passengers and goods.

I traveled with my paranormal team to Chelmsford to see if the trail with the wheel ruts was still there. We also visited the exact location of the original building that housed the Abbott-Downing Company, located on South Main Street in Concord. Then we went to Manchester to see if the energy from the early stagecoach lines there remained. As we walked the stage line heading from Chelmsford toward Billerica, we saw that a partial span of the dirt path still had the recognizable ruts cut into it. We decided to test the area for paranormal activity with the use of an EVP recorder. (EVP is the acronym for Electronic Voice Phenomena; in other words, the art of recording the voices of the dead.) As silly as it might sound, I asked only one question: "Did any Concord Coaches travel on this stagecoach line?"

In Concord, I again asked the same question, only once, in front of what was the Abbott-Downing Company. In Manchester, my team and I stood in the middle of Elm Street, right in the middle of the city, and I repeated the question. We later regrouped to listen to the EVPs. What we heard on tape amazed us. In each location, there was a voice saying only one simple word: *yes*. In Chelmsford, the voice had an Irish brogue. In Manchester and Concord, we received the French-Canadian reply of *oui*.

I didn't feel the that spirits on the old stagecoach lines needed to be healed. They seemed to have transitioned well from coach to car.

UNDERGROUND RAILROAD

A Silent Journey

To understand the complexity of the Underground Railroad and its impact on the Merrimack Valley, one must look to the historical data on the evolution of slavery in the western hemisphere. In the 1440s, Africans were being enslaved by Portugal for use on its sugar plantations. By the sixteenth century, a more organized system of slavery had developed in the Caribbean and Americas, with great influence from Western European nations. Amerindians, natives of the western hemisphere sent for use as slaves in America, and indentured white laborers were priceless commodities in the New World. Over time, and through close contact with the Europeans, the Amerindian population decreased almost to extinction.

Bishop Bartolome de las Casas of Spain fought for the rights of Amerindians and appointed the Spanish government as "Protector of the Indians." This protection did not extend to Africans. Casas was vehemently against all Africans, to such an extent that he endorsed their enslavement to meet the labor demands of his country.

The Triangle Trade, also known as the transatlantic slave trade, brought the transporting and relocating of Africans to the Western Hemisphere. From 1600 to the late 1800s, the slave trade reached its height. In 1619, the first ship of African indentured servants arrived in Jamestown, Virginia. It was not until 1641 that Massachusetts sanctioned the enslavement of all Africans. Other colonial states soon followed suit and ordered all Africans into bondage for life.

Escaping bondage was a dangerously daring feat but not impossible. The outcome of the escape was never what the escapee intended. There was no pot of gold, no freedom for the slaves. The outcome was dismal at best. Still, running away was probably better than being beaten half to death and standing by as your family members were sold to distant landowners. It was a no-win situation for the enslaved; that is, until the advent of the Underground Railroad.

The Underground Railroad was allegedly started in 1786, when Quakers in Philadelphia helped a group of runaway slaves from Virginia reach freedom. In 1787, Isaac Hopper, a brilliant and strong Quaker teen, organized a group of Quakers that helped runaway slaves by providing them with hiding places, food and clothing. In the following years, the system Isaac created with the help of his Quaker friends was being used in many different states to assist and aid runaway slaves on their journeys to freedom.

The term *Underground Railroad* has storybook origins. It has been told that in 1831, Tice Davis ran away from his plantation owner. He was hidden by John Rankin, a white abolitionist from Ohio. Davis's owner found Davis and chased him to the Ohio River. That's when Davis disappeared into thin air. The owner was quoted as saying that Davis must have gone off on some unknown underground road.

The controversy of slavery split the nation between North and South in the late 1850s. Neither side was willing to compromise, and they launched a war of enormous consequence. This was a time of events like the Kansas-Nebraska Act, which created the states of Kansas and Nebraska and gave their residents the right to choose if they wanted slavery; the Dred Scott case of 1857, in which the Supreme Court ruled that people of African descent and their descendants were not protected under the United States Constitution and were never allowed to be United States citizens; *Uncle Tom's Cabin*, the antislavery novel by Harriet Beecher Stowe that, according to Abraham Lincoln, started the Civil War; and the Harpers Ferry raid of October 16, 1859, in which John Brown and his supporters captured the United States Armory/Arsenal at Harpers Ferry. Frederick Douglass once said that the raid on Harpers Ferry was the first act of war in the Civil War. All of these events added fuel to the fire of unrest.

When the Civil War started in 1861, there was a marked exodus of slaves from the South using the Underground Railroad. Many of these slaves joined the Union ranks and fought for their freedom. There were 180,000 African American soldiers and spies who helped the Union forces win the Civil War. The Thirteenth Amendment to the United States Constitution immediately freed over 4,000,000 slaves from bondage. Freedom from bondage should mean exactly that, that the enslaved were free to go any- and everywhere they chose within the continental United Sates. But in an era with no computers or TV to spread the news, and one full of people with wills of their own, the concept of slaves being free, however legal, was often dismissed. Prejudice was alive and well, even in the so-called free states.

Frederick Douglass was invited to speak at a church in Pittsfield, New Hampshire, by the Massachusetts Anti-Slavery Society. Frederick wrote in his autobiography that when he arrived in Pittsfield, his sponsors, Mr. and Mrs. Hilles, were very cruel to him. They were so cruel, in fact, that they made him walk the entire two miles to the church to give his lecture, which Mr. Hilles did not attend. They broke for lunch, and no food was offered to Mr. Douglass. After the service, Douglass was once again left on his own to walk back to town. It was raining, and he saw the same cemetery he had passed on his way to the church. He ventured into the cemetery, sat down and thought: death is the only barrier to discrimination.

When word got out about Douglass's treatment at the lecture, U.S. senator Moses Norris Jr. went out in search of Douglass and found him soaked to the bone. He offered Douglass food and his home to rest in. Not all people in New Hampshire thought like Senator Norris, however. New Hampshire's only president, Franklin Pierce, signed the Fugitive Slave Act on September 18, 1850, and extended the boundaries of slavery westward. The Fugitive Slave Act required that all runaway slaves be brought back to their respective owners. This included slaves who lived in the free states. When a slave was returned to his or her master, he or she was usually beaten, sometimes to death.

Merrimack Valley had its fair share of safe houses to protect slaves on their journey north to freedom. As I researched the Underground Railroad in the Merrimack Valley, I did so from a personal perspective. My own family was enslaved and traveled along the route of the Underground Railroad. A sad history unfolded in front of my eyes as I continued to read the horrific tales of the survivors traveling to be free. To write about all of the wonderful people who stood tall in the face of prejudice and helped these weary travelers on their journey would require a book in itself. So I decided to focus on two specific locations here in the Merrimack Valley, each with its own rich history and legacy as a shelter to the thousands who traveled the lines of the Underground Railroad. The first location is the home of Reverend Humphrey Moore in Milford, New Hampshire, and the second is Stonehenge in Salem, New Hampshire.

The Reverend Humphrey Moore Home

Milford, New Hampshire

Milford is a lovely town in the southern part of New Hampshire. Incorporated in 1794, it had greater tolerance for abolition than many of its sister communities.

Reverend Humphrey Moore came to Milford in 1802. It is said that he was the first settled clergyman in the town at the First Congregational Church. Reverend Moore's salary as a minister, as well as all of the church's expenses, were paid completely by the taxpayers of that town. Reverend Moore served as minister from 1802 until 1836. In 1820, a law was passed that stated that one was not required to pay taxes on a church of which one was not a member. In 1830, the law was changed to state that no money from taxpayers would be used to support churches.

In 1820, Reverend Humphrey Moore purchased land, tore down the old Jonathan Grimes Tavern and built a home of enormous proportions. The home was considered one of the premier homes of its day.

Reverend Humphrey Moore, antislavery supporter. *Photo courtesy of the Milford Historical Society.*

The homestead of Reverend Humphrey Moore, Elm Street, Milford, New Hampshire. *Photo courtesy of the Milford Historical Society.*

Reverend Moore was an abolitionist, and his home was regularly used as a safe haven for slaves during their trek northward. He was also an intricate part of the antislavery convention, which took place in Milford at Eagle Hall on January 4 and 5, 1843. The convention hosted famous abolitionist speakers such as William Lloyd Garrison, Wendell Phillips, Parker Pillsbury, Nathan P. Rogers, C.L. Remond, Abbey Kelly, Stephen S. Foster, George Latimer and Frederick Douglass. The legendary Hutchinson singers from Milford took the stage for the event. The Hutchinson singers were world renowned for their antislavery songs and poetry.

Reverend Moore's home is located on Elm Street in Milford, next to the Souhegan River, and has been converted into apartments. It is a large brick Colonial with expansive wing additions, thirty feet in length, attached to either side of the main house. These wings were made of white wood and housed servants on one side and dignitaries on the other. There was a basement, but it was positioned under the main part of the home. Beneath the wings of the home was a dirt floor.

Many historians have said that there was a visible entrance to a tunnel in Reverend Moore's home, but they didn't know where it was located. I conducted interviews with people around the town of Milford, and a conversation with one woman stood out. She is a volunteer at the Milford Historical Society. She told me that as a child she had heard stories of a tunnel that came off the river and into the home and that children used to play in it. I asked where exactly it was located, and she said she didn't know for sure, but it must have been somewhere out back near the river.

What I did next was reported in many newspapers here in New Hampshire. I documented my research and filmed live streaming video of my paranormal investigation of Reverend Moore's home and property. My videographer, Bob, and I took a long hard look at the home and property to determine where the tunnel might have been. The original home had a barn situated directly behind it, but it doesn't exist anymore. The majority of the land has been sold and is now a recreational park for the people of Milford. The topographical reference to the property has changed so much in recent years with major construction that if there was a tunnel, it has most likely collapsed.

In the basement of the reverend's home, we both felt strange and had a strong urge to venture under one of the wings. I have learned that when dealing with the paranormal, you must always follow your gut instinct. So we went under the wing of the home. There was clearance of about two and a half feet below the floorboards. That didn't include the two- to three-inch nails that hung down through the floor. As we neared the back of the wing, I noticed a breach in the granite foundation. We peered into the breach and discovered a small room, the floor of which sank an additional four feet. In the room, there was a pegged ladder that led to a removable floor panel. On the other side of the floor panel was another space of about three feet in length and two feet in width.

The current owner of the home, Scott, told me that he wasn't aware of such a room. After looking in the apartment directly over the subbasement room, we realized that the area was walled off. Scott had no idea when he purchased the home that there was a room below ground that had been used to hide slaves.

I recalled that the barn had been positioned directly behind the subbasement room, and it dawned on me that the room and the barn had been connected. My cameraman and I climbed into the secret room. To our astonishment, in the back of the secret room was a rebricked archway facing in the direction of the old barn. Upon further investigation, it became clear that there had been a door at the back of the house leading from the servant's kitchen to the barn. This entrance had stairs that went up to the kitchen. This was the same set of stairs that led out of the secret room. History at this point came alive, and we felt euphoric.

Since we were there for a paranormal investigation, we recorded EVPs and fluctuations in temperature. The readings were all across the board. I captured on my recorder the voice of a child wailing while I was in the subbasement room. You can listen to the voice I recorded by going to my website and looking at the samples. The testing told me that the spirits were active and, I felt, in desperate need of healing. After the spirits gave me their permission to heal them, I performed Reiki while sitting in the subbasement room. I picked Reiki because I wanted to heal the horrible strife of the people who had passed through and sought safety there. After the healing, I rerecorded the measurements to see if the levels were lower and consistent. The room felt very calm, and the readings were steady. I concluded that my healing was a success.

This particular investigation was an extremely emotional one for me. I actually broke down and cried several times as the realization took hold that my own family members had lived in rooms like this.

Stonehenge

Salem, New Hampshire

America's Stonehenge in Salem, New Hampshire, is known for its astronomical calendar and for being one of the oldest structures in America, dating back four thousand years. Its calendar can still forecast solar and lunar events, such as the summer and winter solstices. The area is known for the paranormal groups that investigate its stone outcroppings and hidden crawl spaces. America's Stonehenge also played a well-documented role on the Underground Railroad. There were all kinds of artifacts found on the property relating to slaves and their use of the caves as hiding places. This intrigue alone brought me face to face with some of the oldest structures in the United States and one of the cruelest time periods in our nation's history.

The hill on which America's Stonehenge sits is called Mystery Hill and was originally the property of Jonathan Pattee in the 1800s. Pattee, a retired shoemaker, built his home high atop the hill. It is said that he could see for miles from this vantage point. He was part of a group of abolitionists and a stationmaster for the Underground Railroad. His home was located on Boston Post Road, along the route the slaves used as they traveled north to freedom. The Boston Post Road was the main and most direct way for the slaves to travel, for it went from Boston northward to Manchester and straight up to Canada. Many slaves followed the Big Dipper, sometimes called the Drinking Gourd, to freedom. The word *north* was just another word for freedom.

Jonathan Pattee's property was ideal for hiding from the watchful eyes of bounty hunters and authorities. The caves and small stone buildings that lined his property gave the slaves much-needed shelter and rest before they continued on.

I chose to visit America's Stonehenge during the day because it was during the daytime hours that the slaves hid and suffered the most by being stuffed into cramped, dirty quarters. At night, they were free to travel until they reached the next stop.

My videographer and I reached America's Stonehenge and headed straight for the hidden caves. Inside, I could feel the agony that the slaves felt when hiding in their depths. My meters registered off the charts with electric energy. My cameraman felt as if his chest was being pushed on. This can be a sign of intense paranormal energy that has come into contact with one's own electric field. We documented every inch of the cave and took readings that kept changing. We found the caves to be a hotbed of paranormal activity.

We also recorded measurements outside of the cave, and everything registered within normal environmental limits. My next step was to perform a healing and then retest the area. As in the healing of the slaves at Reverend Moore's home, I used Reiki, but this time when I retested the area, the levels were still going wild. This told me that there was more than one type of spiritual energy in that cave. It is very rare that a healing will not work, but given the fact that this cave has seen activity of all kinds for over four thousand years, it is not surprising.

I am prepared for just about anything when it comes to the paranormal, so I took out my quartz crystal and performed a healing. I then buried it in the cave. This act will continue to promote healing of all kinds of energy, animal and human. I retested the area, and the levels were lower and a little steadier. To determine the true effect of the healing, it will take a few months. I will be back to visit the cave in the fall and will retest then. At that time, I will post an update to this section on my website, www.ccthehuntress.com.

OVER THE RIVER AND THROUGH THE WOODS

Haunted Trails and Waterways

In the 1800s, the Merrimack Valley had a thriving manufacturing base that was expanding and growing rapidly to produce textiles and goods for its diverse population. With the rapid growth of the mills came much-needed jobs for the people of the valley. In the midst of all this rapid growth and expansion was one natural resource that no person, animal or mill could do without. The success of the Merrimack Valley hinged on the water of the Merrimack River.

The canal system of the Merrimack Valley was built to divert flowing water to areas not adjacent to the river to increase the availability of power to the ever expanding mill buildings. The canals and towpaths, with their progressive lock systems, offered boat access and turned the surrounding farming community into a thriving metropolis. Then, ingenuity and technology gave birth to the railroads of America, bringing a rapid end to the canal systems. Some of these waterways sit silent and others have been filled in and brought back to their original states.

Our ever expanding highway and road system did the exact same thing to many of the old country roads and train tracks that connected one town to the next. Some of these were mere animal paths that turned into dirt roads and then railroad tracks. Some were state-of-the-art roadways of their time that were discarded when new and straighter highways took their place. These paths, tracks

An old canal entrance off the Merrimack River. *Photo by Laurel Abagis.*

and old dirt roads are now overgrown and barely recognizable, but they represent a priceless history.

Jonathan Eastman, Ebenezer Eastman, Isaac Chandler and Winthrop Fifield formed and incorporated a business in December 1808 called the Proprietors of the Union Locks and Canal. They intended to clear the land near the Merrimack River and to construct much-needed locks for the easy passage of boats and barges from Merrimack to Manchester, New Hampshire. They created six canals total in New Hampshire. They were: Moore's, Coo's, Goff's, Short's, Griffin's and Merrill's. The corporation ran into financial trouble and eventually sold three-quarters of its ownership in 1811 to the Middlesex Canal Company.

The Middlesex Canal was chartered on June 22, 1793, by John Hancock. Construction started in 1795 and continued to 1803, when the twenty-seven-mile canal was completed. Loammi Baldwin was hailed for his excellence in engineering and surveying and proclaimed the project a historic success. Mr. Baldwin was a solider in the American Revolution, and the famed Baldwin Apple of New England was named after him.

The Middlesex Canal was thirty feet wide and three feet deep. There were twenty locks along the canal, each eleven feet wide and eighty feet long. It had a total of eight aqueducts to bring clear drinking water to the cities and towns along its path. As a result of the canal's success, the town of Newburyport, Massachusetts, was no longer the port of choice for bringing goods of trade to the interior of Massachusetts and New Hampshire. Newburyport is a coastal town that sits at the mouth of the Merrimack River, which made it ideal for river travel, despite rough conditions, rocks and strong currents. The canal system was a technological advancement that brought a greater amount of stability to the interior region and expanded the growth of industry in and around the Merrimack River.

I'd like to take you on a little trip down the Merrimack River and share with you some facts about the different canals that line its banks. The Amoskeag Canals at Amoskeag Falls in Manchester, New Hampshire, are filled with mysterious Native American legends. Judge Samuel Blodget received permission to start building the Amoskeag Canal in December 1798. The canal system would take boats and barges around the Amoskeag Falls and bring needed water power to the adjacent textile mills. Shortly after work began on the canal, money ran out, and the legislatures of New Hampshire and Massachusetts employed a lottery to raise money to finish the construction of the canal.

The canal was opened for travel in 1809 with nine working locks. Canal locks are secure, contained structures used to lift or lower boats between areas where the water level differs. These locks were eleven feet wide by one hundred feet long and were laid in the area just below the falls. They extended over a mile and a half to provide easy access to the mills. By 1817, the Middlesex Canal Company had bought the controlling interest in the Amoskeag Canal. This was a good development for the canal, for the financial drain of upkeep and repairs was endless.

The Pawtucket Canal system in Lowell, Massachusetts, was built in 1792 and consisted of 9,000 feet of canal dug around the Pawtucket Falls. This project was completed in 1796 by the Proprietors of Locks and Canals on the Merrimack River. The

Pawtucket Canal Locks were rebuilt in 1822 with an increase in size to 25 feet wide and 1,155 feet long. But by the time 1841 arrived, the locks were again reduced to a mere 12 feet wide for boats. The Pawtucket Canal had a total of seven locks.

The Lawrence Canal in Lawrence, Massachusetts, was one mile in length and had a series of locks called lift locks to overcome the steep drop of over twenty-nine feet in the water level at one section of the canal. These locks were a stout twenty feet wide by one hundred feet long. They also included mitered gates, or a set of gates that closed off the entrance and exit to allow safe passage. In 1845, the locks were rebuilt by the Essex Company, along with the Great Stone Dam. This dam, forty feet in height and built of stone and bedrock, was used to re-form the canal for use as water power by the mills. To this day, the Great Stone Dam has never needed repairs. Due to lack of use and new technological advances, the locks were filled in with dirt in 1960.

I've heard stories about whispering, soft howls and shadowy figures along these three canals. Given their locations, visiting them in the dark is downright scary. But true to my cause, I tested each of the canals. I measured for fluctuation in my readings but found none. I thought this odd because of the great stress put on the animals that pulled the barges along the canals. The only thing I did pick up was in the pictures I took. Each canal's location had an unusually high number of orbs in the pictures. I do believe there was paranormal activity, based on my pictures, but for some reason it registered too low for my equipment to pick up. As a psychic medium, I could not feel any spiritual presence. This is the first time in my life that I felt nothing out of the ordinary on an investigation. Since there was nothing out of the ordinary to feel and nothing registered on my instruments, I felt it best to move along without performing a healing. I will be back in the fall to check if anything has changed.

In Merrimack, New Hampshire, down by the river there is a towpath that is still visible and in use to some extent by hikers. I have ventured up and down this particular towpath in Merrimack many times. This is same towpath that was instrumental in delivering goods to the northland and to the textile towns of the Merrimack Valley. A towpath is a road near the water along which animals and humans pulled canalboats and barges. Years ago, I used to ride my ATV on the towpaths, and I had some great times traveling as far

An abandoned road leading to a towpath on the Merrimack River. *Photo by Laurel Abagis.*

as I could looking at the river and fantasizing about the world of yesterday. These towpaths were essential to the growth of the towns and cities of Merrimack Valley.

One night when I was out researching Merrimack's Colonel French, who died on September 4, 1724, in an Indian massacre, I felt uneasy along a portion of the towpath near the Anheuser-Busch manufacturing plant. According to my research, I was in the exact location where French was slain by the Indians. I pulled out my equipment and started to investigate the area for paranormal activity. My heat meter was the first instrument to detect something. I took out my digital camera and saw a set of three bright green vortex strikes in one of the pictures. The other pictures showed orbs and ecto masses. The vortex strikes were in the vicinity where Colonel French's death occurred.

I also conducted an EVP. I don't always get EVPs as clear as I got that night, but when I asked if I was talking to Colonel French, a bold and loud voice came across on the recording and said, "Yes." It was a man's voice with a slight English accent. When conducting EVP testing, the voice of the person you are trying to contact should sound like it came from the particular time period. In other words, if you were trying to contact a gentleman from the 1700s and a man's voice was captured on your recorder using some hip lingo, you could be assured that it was not coming from the 1700s. I believe I captured an EVP from the 1700s. It may or may not have been Colonel French.

When I asked the spirit if it wanted a healing, I got a warm sensation in my heart. This indicated to me that it did, and I performed an appropriate healing. Colonel French had been chased one mile along the towpath and met his death at the hands and knives of the Indians, who had already slain eight of his friends at the mouth of Horseshoe Pond. Taking these facts into consideration, I decided to do a healing using sweet grass. Sweet grass was used in many Native American tribes to cleanse areas. I felt that both the Indians and French needed to be healed together so that their spirits could be freed from the burden of death that still bound them here. I prayed to the north, south, east and west for comfort and understanding of mankind's choices. I planted some of the sweet grass seeds and disbursed the rest to the winds. I bowed my head, and the healing was done.

Upon retesting the area, I found the temperature to be a steady seventy-five degrees with no variations, and the pictures I took showed no orbs or vortex strikes. All was calm and serene. I saw this as a sign of understanding and a healing between two different spirits/cultures in turmoil.

RIP

Rest in Peace

Have you ever given any thought to gravestone epitaphs and art? I want to bring to light some of the more fascinating and humorous epitaphs I have had the pleasure of viewing and discuss the ever-changing decorations on our loved ones' memorial stones.

At one time, people buried their dead in mounds and covered them with piles of stones so the deceased wouldn't climb up out of the grave and haunt them. Gravestones go by many different names: monuments, markers, headstones, tombstones and steles. A stele is a gravestone made of wood or a stone slab whose length is taller than its width. These steles are placed on top of the graves to honor the dead. Some have elaborate inscriptions, and others simply have a name and date. A tombstone was actually the lid of a coffin and was almost always made of stone.

Originally, gravestones were flat, rectangle-shaped stones placed over the actual buried coffin. Today, gravestones are placed at the head of the grave. Footstones were often used in the 1700s to mark the end of a person's coffin in the ground. These footstones rarely had an inscription, usually just an initial and maybe a year of death. The practice of placing a footstone at the end of the grave is still common in the United Kingdom, but is no longer used in the United States.

People would use gravestones as a sign of wealth and importance in the community. The bigger the stone or monument, the wealthier you

Thornton Ferry Cemetery, Merrimack, New Hampshire. *Photo by Bob Abagis.*

were and the better the life you lived. Sometimes a person still very much alive would have a large gravestone erected just to show off his wealth before death.

Gravestones were made of many different types of materials. The earliest were fieldstones. They were found in fields, hence their name, and were easily placed on the grave, but they lacked style and were at times too bumpy to inscribe. In early colonial times, sandstone was the stone of choice and replaced the fieldstone. The problem with sandstone was that in the winter, when rain turned to snow, precipitation would settle in the cracks and creases of the sandstone and freeze. Freezing would expand the stone, and it would literally fall apart. Marble and limestone soon replaced sandstone; both are delightful materials to work with. They're easy to inscribe and hold up better under the elements than wrought iron. However, over time they will start to dissolve, and the inscriptions will become unreadable.

Winged Angel Cemetery, Groveland, Massachusetts. *Photo by CC Carole.*

During the Georgian era (1714–1811), wood was used for gravestones. It was easy to inscribe and decorate but lasted only a short period of time because it rots quickly. Wrought iron was used in the Victorian era of the mid-1850s. This material was easy to inscribe and could be made into the most ornate gravestones, but iron rusts and proved not a good choice in a short period of time. Cast iron, on the other hand, has stood and still stands the test of time. Granite is commonly used for gravestones today because it is extremely hard and durable. It can be carved and inscribed using sandblasting. Intricate designs can be placed on a granite stone with the use of a computer.

The artwork on gravestones is a silent language all to itself. It reflects the life, and sometimes career, of the deceased and can tell you what faith he or she came from. Not all gravestones have artwork; some are simple, with only a name and date of death.

In the seventeenth century, there was widespread use of the death head, or winged angels, as I like to call them. This was a head with wings underneath. Some death heads had hair and some did not. The reason for the hairless heads was the contemporary belief that a person's hair would be burned off by demons after death. Another reason was that one's burdens would be released when one died; hair was a burden, so a hairless winged angel represented the release of human burdens. On the other hand, later in the seventeenth century, hair was a common feature on the winged angels. Views of death had begun to change. The fear of death was replaced with a love of life and God. A full head of hair represented the full life the deceased had on earth and the full life he or she would have in heaven.

In the eighteenth century, little cherubs started to replace the death heads. This again showed a progressive thought process emerging. This little cherub represented a person on his or her way to heaven.

Flowers represented eternal life after death, but if the flowers on the stone were upside down, they meant that life had come to an end. The bearer of this type of flower believed that there was no life after death and everything ceased to exist. Wreaths made of flowers or vines indicated wealth in life and a wealth of greatness when they arrived in heaven.

Some people also put their line of work on their gravestones. The image or symbol for this would be, for example, an anchor for someone who made his living on the sea. Plants on a gravestone indicated a wealthy farmer. Willows used solely on a gravestone told people that the deceased would have everlasting life after death. Urns were used to represent the person who died. Gravestones with both the willow and urn basically said that the person who died would rise again to a life after death.

Epitaphs are inscriptions on the gravestone that give people a glimpse into the life of the deceased. The following are some of my favorite epitaphs:

Matthew Thornton—The Honest Man.

Effie Jean Robinson—Come blooming youths, as you pass by, And on these lines do cast an eye. As you are now, so once was I; As I am now, so must you be; Prepare for death and follow me.

"Honest Man" Matthew Thornton's gravestone, Merrimack, New Hampshire. *Photo by CC Carole.*

Eliza, Sorrowing—Rears This Marble Slab, To Her Dear John, Who Died of Eating Crab.

Robert Phillip—Here I lie at the Chancel door; Here I lie because I am poor; Here I lie as warm as they, The farther the more you pay.

Old Spinster—Returned—Unopened.

Unhappily Married—Here beneath this stone we lie; Back to back my wife and I; And when the angels trump shall trill; If she gets up then I'll lie still.

Cheating Husband—Gone, but not forgiven.

Ezekiel Aikle—Died Age 102. The Good Die Young.

Mary Lefavour—Reader pass on and ne'er waste your time; On bad biography and bitter rhyme. For what I am this cumb'rous clay insures, And what I was, is no affair of yours.

No Name—Cold is my bed, but oh, I love it. For colder are my friends above it.

Jonathan Blake—Here lies the body of Jonathan Blake, Stepped on the gas; instead of the brake.

Thomas Stagg's—That is all.

REFERENCES

Browne, G. Waldo. *Legends of Yesterday.* Manchester, NH: Standard Book Company, 1919.

Lowell Weekly Times. "Gov. Butlers Charges against the Tewksbury Almshouse management." March 1883. Available online at http://www.tewksburyhistoricalsociety.org/Archives/LowellSun/03311883.pdf.

New York Times "Horrible Calamity." January 1860. Available online at http://query.nytimes.com/mem/archive-free/pdf?_r=2&res=9503E5DB173BE53BBC4952DFB766838B679FDE.

Skinner, Charles A. *Myths & Legends of Our Own Land.* Vol. I. London: J.B. Lippincott Company, 1896.

Sultzman, Lee. "First Nations History." Pennacook History. http://www.dickshovel.com/penna.html.

About the Author

Internationally renowned paranormal specialist CC Carole is host of her own paranormal TV show, *CC the Huntress*, on PTN, the Paranormal Television Network/Para-x powered by CBS. CC is a registered Usui and licensed Karuna Reiki master and a professional ghost hunter. She has had advanced multimedia and video production training at ATT Broadband Studios. CC is the co-producer of *Ghost Stories of New England*, and her work has been aired on FOX, WNDS, Comcast, Adelphia, Metrocast and other cable outlets, both national and international.

Ms. Carole is a respected contributor and sits on the board of advisors for *Applaud Women* magazine, a diverse and informative women's magazine. She hunts and heals the spirits she comes into contact with. She is a believer that "death does not end suffering." You can see all of this in her television shows, as she uses ancient rituals and common practice energy healing to soothe the souls of the dead. When not hunting and healing ghosts, you can find CC enjoying time with her husband, children and dear pets.

Visit her website for information: www.ccthehuntress.com.

Visit us at
www.historypress.net

www.ingramcontent.com/pod-product-compliance
Lightning Source LLC
Chambersburg PA
CBHW042144160426
43201CB00022B/2403